HOW TO MANAGE YOUR BOARD WHILE YOUR BOARD MANAGES YOU

A Practical Guide To Working Effectively
With a Board For Both New and Experienced CEOs

MARTIN M. COYNE II

ISBN: 1-4392-3927-4
ISBN-13: 9781439239278
Library of Congress Control Number: 2009904129

Visit www.booksurge.com to order additional copies.

To my wife Patrice and our sons

CONTENTS

Introduction
Getting off to a Fast Start

Congratulations! You're the CEO. Your hard work over many years has paid off, and you have reached a pinnacle of success that few achieve. As a high performer, you're probably eager to get on with your new job but take some time to celebrate! Enjoy that glass of champagne, mingle with colleagues and friends, and truly appreciate what you've accomplished. It is a great achievement to be named CEO of a company. Celebrate your success and revel in what you have achieved.

To make it to the top, you have developed a set of skills and experiences necessary to be named the CEO. You now get to run things your way, at your pace, and in your style. Lessons learned over many years can be applied according to your best judgment and experience. When your board named you CEO, the members visibly confirmed their belief in your ability to do the job successfully.

Time to Get to Work

In today's world, the time to celebrate is usually cut short by the demands of being CEO. I am always amazed by the questions a new CEO faces when CNBC or the business press interviews them on the day of his or her appointment. Typical questions might be: What is your vision for your company? What are your revenue and earnings targets? What will you do differently from your predecessor? What are the major issues facing your company, and how will you deal with them?

These questions can occur within hours of your appointment. And it's not just the financial press—your management team, employees, and investors may be asking the same questions or at least thinking them. To meet immediate expectations, you will be required to be a prophet, sage, and experienced CEO, and display the Wisdom of Solomon. The challenges you will face in your new role will exceed anything you have ever faced in your business career.

The pressures of being a CEO are intense and never ending. It's highly likely that as the months and years go by, you'll experience the loneliness of being at the top. The time demands you will face from all your constituencies will challenge, even derail the best time-management processes you learned over the years. Your activities must be prioritized as never before, so that you extract the maximum value from every minute you spend on the job and every interaction you have.

It's critical that you develop a clear operating framework; not only for your first days but also for every year you're in this key position. You'll constantly be challenged to develop a clear vision and goals for your organization while simultaneously focusing on business operations and strategy. Your constituencies will demand clear and continual communication about current performance, your expectations, and your future plans.

Working Smart

There have been many books and articles written to help CEOs develop plans for leadership success. These books contain valuable information and an operating structure to help them meet business demands in a logical and thoughtful way. The authors of these books have studied new and successful CEOs and the business demands placed on them. They have taken the best of what they've seen and organized the information in a way that will benefit all CEOs.

However, very little has been written about how a CEO can effectively and efficiently structure a successful relationship with their board of directors.

This book is designed to provide the context, framework, and process to help you work effectively with your board from day one and every day you're the CEO. Over the past decade, from my board activities and attending board meetings as a senior executive before becoming a board member, I observed how many CEOs interacted with their boards. I have had the opportunity to work closely with a diverse group of new and highly successful, experienced CEOs as a board chair, lead director, director, committee member, and senior business adviser. I have counseled and mentored new and experienced CEOs on how to work effectively with their boards. I have witnessed firsthand what works and also witnessed actions that jeopardized or inhibited the development of a strong and sustainable relationship between CEOs and their boards.

This book distills my knowledge and observations in an easy-to-read format. If you are a new CEO, the lessons in this book are designed to be helpful in jump-starting your relationship with your board; if you are an experienced CEO, the lessons will help improve your relationship with your board. They will stand the test of time and allow you to constantly assess and enhance your board relationship over time. Hopefully, you'll use this book as a blueprint for developing and maintaining a successful relationship with your board.

This book can also be used as a practical reference guide for senior executives who frequently present to boards or board committees and who aspire to be a CEO one day. It contains the fundamentals of board and board committee focus and processes, as well as the most important issues that directors are keen to discuss. Understanding these issues and governance processes can significantly improve the effectiveness of these senior executives and help them improve their chances for advancement.

Your Board Believes in You

As I noted earlier, you would not be CEO if your board did not have confidence in your ability, skills, and experience. The fact that you have been chosen CEO after thorough vetting by your board indicates the board's confidence in your capability to do the job. They want you to be successful. In short, no CEO is perfect, but your board understands this and is willing to work with you to help you continually improve.

The knowledge that your board believes in you, trusts you, and wants you to be successful is a firm foundation on which to build a strong and long-lasting relationship with your board. Don't underestimate the importance of their confidence in you and their desire to help you succeed as CEO.

You Already Have the Skills

One important skill set that you learned on your journey to becoming CEO was managing and communicating in a formal business organizational structure. To be successful in previous leadership positions, you needed to learn how to work downward, across, and upward in your organization. By this I mean that you learned to effectively manage downward to those who reported to you. You communicated a vision, clear expectations, and provided feedback on performance. You also had to learn to effectively work across boundaries, business units, and functional areas to achieve results and win the respect and cooperation of your peers. Finally, you needed to effectively manage and communicate upward to your supervisor. To reach the top, you learned to mange effectively in all three directions, albeit probably not without some bruises along the way.

As CEO, your supervisor is your board of directors. Many of the lessons that you learned about managing upward as you assumed positions of increasing responsibility over the years are still applicable to working with your board. The effective communication, prioritization, and interpersonal skills that enabled you to become CEO remain valuable when used correctly.

Getting Off to a Fast Start with Your Board

As a CEO, one of the dangers you face is distraction from developing optimal board relationships due to competing pressures from other important constituencies. Your employees, shareholders, financial community, suppliers, customers, government regulators, and local community issues may collectively present demands that can distract you from improving your relationship with your board. Each of these constituencies wants to make their case early in your tenure and may seek a disproportionate share of your valuable time. Their demands in some cases may present you with conflicting and complicated issues that absorb large amounts of time. There is no easy way to avoid these conflicting demands, so hard work and long hours are part of the job.

Spending time thinking about and planning how to work with your board can easily fall to a lower priority or may even be totally overlooked. You must work hard to prevent this from happening.

It is critical that you set the right operating style with your board from the beginning in two key areas: how you will relate to your board and what you expect from your board members. Successfully addressing both topics requires a clear understanding of board duties, focus, and operating processes. Building on this knowledge, you can then conceive and implement a focused plan to continually build an open and trusting relationship with your board.

When you're successful, you will view your board as a valuable resource and not as an adversary. While the board is your supervisor, they must also be your colleagues, advisers, and mentors. I'll discuss later some the frictions that can arise between you and your board. Although the road is never perfectly smooth, your success depends on developing a strong working relationship with your board and seeing them as allies.

Five Fundamental Principles

This book contains lessons drawn from observing effective CEOs deal with their boards as well as lessons from those who have made rookie mistakes. Its purpose is to help you apply the knowledge and experience of successful CEOs and to avoid the mistakes that others have made. When applied successfully, this knowledge should help you get off to a fast start and sustain a productive working relationship with your board. Some of the suggestions and practices in this book may seem obvious to you. However, some CEOs neglect or ineffectively implement them. Working constructively with your board is far from an exact science. The suggestions in this book can be applied immediately and also continually over time to improve your relationship with your board. This will help strengthen your performance as CEO and ultimately make you more successful.

Five fundamental principles form the foundation of this book.

1. Understand your board's focus and expectations.
2. Provide timely, accurate, and relevant information to your directors.
3. Establish effective two-way communication with your board and individual directors.
4. Develop a robust, continual personal assessment and feedback process.
5. Use continual change as an opportunity to enhance your board relationship.

These principles, when implemented successfully, create strong and effective governance processes and make for a positive and powerful relationship between you and your board. You will personally benefit from this improved teamwork, as will your employees and shareholders.

There are questions in the appendix to help you reflect on your current board relationship and assess your understanding and adherence to these principles.

Benefits of a Strong Board Relationship

There are two significant benefits to establishing a strong working relationship with your board. The first is that you gain the capability to tap into the experience and knowledge of your directors and that will help you make better business decisions. The second is that you'll find your board to be much more supportive and less adversarial in their interactions with you.

An engaged and supportive board can help you get off to a fast start as CEO and then help you to grow personally and professionally. Implementing the concepts in this book can help you increase your effectiveness over time, so that as your company grows, you continue to develop as a successful CEO. As your board evolves, your relationship with the directors can remain positive and constructive, and that will create the most value for shareholders.

From day one, you have the opportunity to demonstrate that you're accessible to your directors, value their input, and will use their experience and counsel. You have the opportunity to create an environment in which their issues or concerns can be discussed openly and honestly. You can be candid in discussions and not feel that you must have answers all the time. In this type of environment, it's permissible and desirable to say what you think about a problem, and ask for the board's help and advice, so that you can come up with the best solution.

Even if you have been the CEO for a while and don't have this type of working relationship with your board, it's never too late to start. Let's get going!

Developing Your Plan

To help you develop your own personal plan to manage your relationship with your board, the book is divided into three sections. Each section builds off the preceding one, but each can also serve separately as a resource.

1. Understanding Board Governance

Every board is different in terms of size, experience, governance processes, personalities, and relationships. To be successful, you must understand these differences, why they are important, and how they can affect the plan you ultimately develop.

Chapters 1 through 8 provide an overview of the governance environment, the focus of your board, and an overview of the most important board committees. A clear understanding of how and why your board functions as it does enhances your ability to create a sustainable plan that gets you off to a fast start.

2. Developing a Successful Plan

Chapters 9 and 10 review the most important planning components and identify the tensions that can develop in the process. To work effectively with your board, you'll need to work effectively with the individual directors, board committees, and the board as a whole. Working effectively demands a clear board and management focus on important governance topics, achieving the right level of communication frequency and content, and establishing the right governance culture.

To track the effectiveness of your plan, you must create a robust and candid feedback process with your board. This process is both formal and informal. The culture for gaining this feedback must be established and cultivated continually.

3. Improving Your Board Relationship

Your initial plan and its evolution are critical to establishing the right relationship with your board. However, every change that occurs in board membership and committee structure has the potential to markedly change board interactions and your relationship with your board. Chapter 11 helps you to apply the lessons in the preceding chapters to strengthen your board relationships.

Introspective questions in the appendix will help you organize your thoughts, assess your progress, and suggest opportunities for improvement to your plan. These questions will help you evaluate the book's five foundation principles and other important board relationship topics covered in the various chapters. Periodic reflection on these questions will provide a structured framework to help you evaluate your current board relationship. Opportunities for meaningful improvement will become clear and actionable.

PART ONE:

UNDERSTANDING BOARD GOVERNANCE

Chapter One
Your Governance Environment

All boards have been faced with continually changing legal and regulatory requirements and shareholder pressures. In years past, the primary role of a successful board was defined as implementing two primary legal and fiduciary requirements: the duty of care and the duty of loyalty. These fundamental duties, while still a core governance requirement, have been expanded to ensure compliance with new regulatory requirements and also affected by activist shareholder initiatives.

Board Duties

Simply put, the duty of care requires directors to act on an informed basis with the same level of care and diligence that a reasonable person would exercise under similar circumstances. To achieve this, the board needs to be fully informed and engaged in a thoughtful decision-making process.

The duty of loyalty requires directors to refrain from deriving a benefit from a transaction that's not generally available to all shareholders. This means that a director has to put the interests of shareholders ahead of any personal interests and the interests of employees and other constituencies. There are other duties, such as those of disclosure and confidentiality, but the duties of care and loyalty guide most of a board's behavior.

In reality, the duties of care and loyalty seem straightforward and relatively easy to implement by directors. However, the inherent challenge lies in translating the legal language into effective board governance.

For example, under the duty of care, the board is to act on an informed basis, but the CEO is the real expert on the business. Who besides the CEO understands as much about the business and the ramifications of each business decision? How can a board know enough to question what a CEO wants to do? How does a board member, who might be far less knowledgeable, have the audacity to question the decisions of the CEO? This is what can cause tension in today's boardroom. Directors are implementing a broader definition of the duty of care while some CEOs are fiercely resisting any kind of challenge to their authority or autonomy. The tension is compounded when the board members who had been selected by the CEO and routinely approved whatever the CEO requested now become the inquisitors.

To eliminate these tensions, an effective CEO needs to work in partnership with his or her board to achieve the right balance. You and your team are responsible for creating long-term value for your shareholders in an ethical and socially responsible manner. The board is responsible for ensuring that the plans are in place and resourced properly to create value for shareholders. The board also needs to be confident that key business risks are understood and that actions are in place to mitigate these risks.

There is a clear need for CEOs to understand how the new governance requirements are changing their board's expectations. CEOs need to apply proven management techniques and processes that will help them work successfully with their board.

Compliance Versus Guidance

The optimal governance balance requires the correct mix of ensuring compliance while still providing the proper level of guidance. Tom Perkins, of Kleiner Perkins Caufield and Byers, described in the *Wall Street Journal* two types of boards: a *compliance board* and a *guidance board*. According to Perkins, a compliance board focuses on ensuring that all corporate governance mandates are met. A guidance board focuses on providing input and counsel to the CEO and management team.

A board that is either a compliance board or a guidance board carried to extreme usually becomes a weakness and makes it difficult for any CEO to be successful. In actual practice, you must continually provide information and feedback to your board to help them strike the proper balance.

The perfect balance is rarely found, and a steady-state equilibrium between the two governance extremes is difficult to sustain. Your relationship with your board may operate more like a pendulum. In the optimal state, the pendulum oscillates slowly, in a relatively small arc around the center, and rarely moves to either extreme of compliance or guidance. Under these conditions, compliance can be achieved with the proper level of guidance. This balanced compliance-governance model will be the most help to you and create the greatest value for the stockholders over time. Only rarely should your relationship with the board need to deviate far from the center.

As you interact with your board and its individual directors, continually assess where your board falls on the spectrum of compliance and guidance. Help them to strike the proper balance through your actions and the feedback you provide to them. Your efforts in this area can create an energizing work environment for you, while also helping you to be successful.

Every Situation Is Unique

The strategies in this book are designed to be applicable to the diverse and continually changing circumstances that each CEO faces. In reality, the interaction between each CEO and his or her board is unique. However, there are common lessons, processes and strategies you can use to build a successful relationship with your board. The differences, diversity, and continual change you experience can actually be positive if you manage your board relationship properly. If you fail to interact well with your board, or if you do not understand your board and individual directors, your relationship can get quite tense and at times cause personal failure.

Boards are composed of highly successful people trying to implement good governance processes in a constantly changing business environment. It's important to remember that people will be people! Every board is different and every CEO is different. Governance processes will change and your business results and challenges in an ever-changing, competitive environment will be different each quarter and each year.

These differences in human interactions, different approaches to the governance process and changes in the business climate can be powerful and energizing if understood and managed properly. *Vive la difference!*

Every Board Is Different

Director experiences, working relationships, egos, and the perspectives of each director are different. The average board has eight to twelve members. Let's assume an average of ten directors, plus you as CEO. This means there are eleven intelligent and successful people in a board meeting, and three to four people at each committee meeting. Each individual has a breadth and depth of experience that has made him or her successful and a valuable, contributing board member.

Individual perspectives on issues will be different based on each individual's personal experience. Interactions will be different based on who is on each committee and who is present for board meetings. Sometimes the absence of one director at a board or committee meeting can significantly change the meeting dynamics, discussion, and flow.

Directors, being human, will react differently according to the circumstances. They will interact differently depending who is in the room and the subjects being discussed. They will also act differently due to external forces. During the economic crisis of 2008-09, I have witnessed directors who would, under normal circumstances assemble facts and make decisions rapidly, now take hours debating and discussing a major decision. Some of their comments were prudent, based on the uncertainty of the times. However, much of their time and effort was spent trying to find more clarity when that was impossible. In some cases, final decisions took months or several board meetings. The opportunity cost was high and the additional work generated little value.

Over time, I have been continually amazed and surprised at the subtle differences in the quality and content of board discussions when a particular director is absent. Sometimes, the discussion dramatically improves, while in other cases valuable perspective is lost. Take the time to observe these changes so you can better work with your directors and help make your board discussions as valuable as possible.

Stage of Governance Evolution

Governance processes are in a constant state of evolution. The pace of change in the last few years has accelerated. Each board is in a different place on their governance journey and will continually evolve. Governance processes at each company will be at a different state of maturity and the key areas of board emphasis may vary.

Individual directors also bring their own experience on governance to each board and committee meeting. Some are also directors at other companies and are influenced by those governance practices. These perspectives can be quite varied and create valuable, robust discussions.

The real power of these governance differences lies in your ability to work closely with your directors to harness the best practices they have learned. If you take the time to understand how your directors work effectively with other CEOs, you can help guide your board toward a similar relationship with you.

State of Current Business Performance

Board meeting behavior and discussions are heavily influenced by each director's level of understanding of business issues and current business performance. As we'll discuss later, two of the primary responsibilities of a board are reviewing and approving the annual operating plan and the long-term strategy of your company.

Business performance versus plan is usually evaluated quarterly. The competitive environment, which influences strategy, is constantly changing over the short and long term. Current performance must always to be placed in the context of previous performance and expected future performance. This context creates differences in board expectations and also provides a yardstick your board will use to track performance. Again, no two companies are in the exact same position in their marketplace, so expect subtle but tangible differences.

Every CEO is Different

You are unique and have been chosen to be CEO because of your uniqueness. You have qualities that your board deems critical to ensure your company's success.

You also will differ from other CEOs in terms of time in position, time with your company, and the relationship with your board. Some of you will be first-time CEOs; others will have been a CEO at another company. Some will be well known to their boards because you worked your way up through the ranks and gained exposure to their board over several years; others will be outside hires, working with your board for the first time.

It's important to understand your starting relationship with your board because you can use this as one of the pillars of building a strong relationship with them. It's also important to understand the focus and activities of your full board, as well as how it uses committees to subdivide some of the its work.

Chapter Two
Annual Operating Plan

Typically, boards focus on four core areas: annual operating plan oversight, strategy oversight, CEO succession planning and executive development, and risk management. Let's explore each of these areas in more detail to provide additional perspective on board expectations and processes.

Effective business planning and plan execution is a requirement for every successful CEO. In today's world of heightened investor expectations, predictable operating performance is mandatory. This predictability needs to be achieved without managing the quarterly numbers as has occurred in some companies in the past.

Plan Development and Approval Process

By the middle of the fourth quarter of your fiscal year, your board will expect a preliminary review of your draft annual operating plan for the coming year. This initiates the process of review and discussion of your annual operating plan. The draft plan is based on ten months actual performance with your best estimate for the remaining two months of the year. The focus is on current year-to-date performance, your estimate for the balance of the year, financial run rates, and your planning assumptions for the coming year. These are quantified into a preliminary profit and loss (P&L) and cash flow projection for the upcoming year.

Expect your board to discuss and probe your assumptions, business objectives, tactical plans, and expected financial results. Their questions will help them to understand your thought process, the aggressiveness of your proposed goals, the risks involved, and your assumptions about the market and competitor activity. Early in the first quarter of the new fiscal year, when the board is satisfied that you have prepared and committed to a realistic and achievable annual operating plan that is resourced properly, they will approve it. The board role then changes to one of monitoring achievement of the plan. A significant part of each board meeting will be devoted to reviewing the company's performance versus its operating plan.

Your company's annual operating plan is fundamental to creating shareholder value. The board's job is to review your plan and use their collective experience to provide feedback and suggestions to improve the plan.

You should make sure that before approving your plan, the board has one or two preliminary sessions to become well-grounded in the business issues and have adequate time to discuss and reflect on your proposed plan. During these sessions, the board's role is to provide specific feedback that you can address in your final plan.

At year end, after the final numbers are in, you and your team update next year's preliminary plan, incorporating board feedback and the previous year's final financials. You present this plan at the first meeting of the new fiscal year— usually at the January board meeting. Ideally, if this process works correctly, the January board review becomes a fine-tuning exercise. The assumptions in the plan have been vetted twice. You have previously reached agreement with the board on target growth percentages, revenue, earnings, and cash flow in absolute dollars as well as acceptable percentage ratios for gross margin, SG&A, and R&D investments.

As part of your final plan review, you should identify the key drivers of business performance in the coming year along with the critical tactics you will implement for each driver. Additionally, to help the board assess your plan's risks, you should review its upsides and downsides.

This final review should go fairly routinely unless something dramatic has happened in the past two months. This could occur in two areas. First, the performance in the last two months of the preceding year could be significantly different than the forecast—either much higher or lower. Secondly, some important event could have occurred in the markets in which you compete. Examples could be an acquisition, divestiture, significant competitive business initiative, or a major new product launch. In either case, you need to make sure the board thoroughly understands what has changed, the reasons behind the change, and the implications for your business and annual plan.

Monitoring Plan Performance

At each board meeting, an important agenda topic will be to review performance versus plan on a quarterly basis and also assess year-to-date performance. It is important to reach agreement with your board on the performance criteria you will use to monitor the success of your plan. These criteria fall into two categories. The first are the obvious financial results from the P&L, balance sheet, and cash flow statements. Expect your board to look at performance in absolute dollars, percentage changes over prior periods, and key ratios of performance compared to either revenue or earnings from operations.

You should also propose a set of measurements that track performance in critical categories such as shareholder value creation, customer satisfaction, and key human resource issues. One method to keep the board focused on relevant information is to track a series of key performance indicators (KPIs) that track these three important categories of business performance. Ideally, there should be three to five measurements for each of the three categories. Take the time to review these with your board, discussing why you have chosen them and why they will be effective indicators of plan performance.

Using a simple stop light chart technique to track performance versus plan, you can manage the board's business performance discussions by succinctly reporting on performance versus each KPI and discussing remedial plans for any shortfalls. This approach has proven to be an excellent way for a CEO to manage and focus board discussions while avoiding spending time on less relevant topics. Proactive and open communication to your board on these performance indicators can alleviate its concerns and anxiety that you are ignoring or insufficiently addressing important operational details.

As part of their fiduciary responsibility, your board needs to clearly understand business performance. If there are shortfalls, they need to understand what corrective actions you will implement to get back on plan. Obviously, you will need to explain the reasons for any shortfalls to the board, but explanations alone will not be sufficient. Your board will expect specific, concrete steps to achieve missed performance commitments. Conversely, if you are exceeding the plan and results could be further improved through additional investment, the board will expect proposals for incremental spending or investments.

Assessing Plan Performance

Achieving your operating commitments, how they were achieved, and whether you adhered to your corporate values will be major components of your board's assessment of your performance as CEO. In short, what was accomplished and how was it accomplished?

Performance versus plan shapes your corporate guidance to the external world. Publicly traded companies customarily provide some level of quarterly or at least annual guidance. Achievement of this guidance is a reflection of many things, including the quality and aggressiveness of your annual plan. Specifically, does your plan utilize your assets to the best possible extent to create value for your shareholders? Secondly, if your plan is aggressive and realistic, how will your performance compare to competitors? Are you gaining or losing market share? Are you growing at the rate of market growth or growing faster than the market? Is price competition that would decrease gross margins accelerating?

The investment community will assess your performance on these and other dimensions and decide whether to invest in your company. This has a direct correlation to the value you create for your shareholders.

Summary

The annual operating planning process is one of the primary responsibilities for you and your board. It is your job as CEO to effectively lead the planning process with your management team. While you may chose to solicit feedback and input from individual board members, it is your job to prepare the plan.

Your board's role is to thoroughly review your proposed plan, understand the planning details and assumptions, and challenge you and your team to ensure that the plan is aggressive, achievable, and utilizes your resources to the best possible extent.

Your board will use the annual operating planning process and your performance in achieving the plan as key measurement criteria for the evaluation of your performance as CEO, as well as the performance of members of your management team. It is beneficial for you and your team to tap into board members' experience before completion of the final plan to ensure that the plan you present is as strong as possible.

Chapter Three
Business Strategy

Strategic planning is another critical role for every CEO and board. In my conversations with board members, there is a unanimous desire to spend more time understanding and discussing their company's strategy. Many directors have told me that their boards struggle with the strategic planning process. Finding time for periodic reviews and keeping up with changes in the competitive environment can also be a challenge.

Because markets, customers, and competitors are never static, strategic planning is vital for sustained business success. However, many board meetings spend too much time reviewing operating performance at the expense of robust discussions of strategy. This balance between operational and strategy discussions is like driving a car. Operational performance looks out the rear window, while strategy looks at what is on the road ahead. As CEO, help your board to strike the proper balance between looking forward and looking backward.

Remember that your directors are not active daily in your business and have only limited time to devote to it. Leading board strategy discussions, providing relevant information, and reviewing your strategy can be a challenge for you and your management team. But to most effectively help you, your board desires and needs continuous discussion of strategy and the long-term outlook for your business.

The board expects that you and your management team will develop a long-term view of your business, anticipate competitive activity and technology advances, and invest in technologies and competencies to achieve sustainable competitive advantage and create increased value for your shareholders.

Absent a strategy to create additional shareholder value, a board is left with two alternatives. First, it may conclude that the CEO and the management team are incapable or not sufficiently creative to continuously and profitably grow the business. If this is the case, it has no alternative than to begin candid and objective discussions about the company's executive leadership. Alternatively, the board may conclude that they have the right CEO and management team, but, for whatever reason, the business cannot continue to grow profitably and therefore shareholder value will decline. If this is the case, they have two options: They can return value to the shareholders either by selling assets, divesting the company, or use some other mechanism to return value to the owners. Or they will look to you to provide an investment plan to acquire new products or technology or an acquisition to increase shareholder value.

These alternatives are complex and difficult, but one important fact remains—your board needs to review, understand, challenge, and agree upon a long-term strategy for your company. If you and your board are successful, you have a roadmap to generate sustained long-term shareholder value. If you fail to develop and execute a strong plan or fail to return value to your shareholders, you and your board have failed. Today, with shareholders becoming increasingly active, this failure can easily result in replacing the CEO. These are the blunt and harsh realities of being a CEO or board member today!

Plan Development and Approval Process

Many boards use the mid-year or July board meeting as the forum to review, discuss, and approve the three-year strategic plan. The timing is appropriate because it fits well into the fiscal year. In January, the board reviews and approves your annual operating plan for the current year. In reality, this is the foundation of your three-year-plan. In July, you are updating this plan to incorporate actual performance from six months of the current year and then looking out over the next three years.

Practically, this means that you and your board are reviewing the overall state of the business, operating results, competition, and the productivity of investments in technology, infrastructure and people every six months. From a board perspective, this is a realistic time frame to observe business and industry changes and to provide you with the opportunity to discuss management's plans to address these changes.

In your April board meeting, or the one immediately before your strategy review, you should work with your board to identify and structure the key strategic issues that you will address in July. Proactively propose to the board those issues that you believe to be the most critical to address. Solicit input from your board on other issues they may want you to also address in the strategy discussions.

Your objective is to gain agreement with your board on the issues that will make the strategic discussions most valuable. Taking time for this before the strategy review helps to frame and focus the discussions for maximum value.

Remember that the three-year strategic plan review is the first look your board will have at next year's potential operating plan financials. In practice, these financials are an extension of the current year's six-month actual performance, plus an estimate for the remaining six months. The feedback and reaction you receive can be very helpful as the current year unfolds and the next year's operating plan is developed, as we discussed in chapter 2.

You and your team must lead this strategic planning process. None of your board members are close enough to your business to develop your strategy, nor should they. However, feel free to utilize the expertise that resides on your board. Most directors are experienced enough to understand and appreciate a sound long-range plan. Conversely, they have all seen poor plans.

Each of your board members should understand the distinction between providing advice on a strategy and owning strategy development. Each of your directors should be available to help without getting in the way or usurping your authority.

At your July board meeting, the focus will be on reviewing, discussing, and challenging your proposed strategy. Don't expect your board will to do a cursory review and move on to the next agenda item. Expect your board to take their responsibility seriously. Ideally, you should send your strategic plan to them at least a week before the meeting to provide them adequate time to review and digest the strategy. Assume that they will read it carefully and be prepared to offer their comments, reactions, and advice.

Monitoring Your Strategy

There are fundamentally several ways a board can track the thoughtfulness and performance of your strategic plan and the process used to develop the plan. The first is the consistency of the planning assumptions, market description, business performance, and growth rates that the board sees in your quarterly operating reviews. If assumptions are constantly changing, market share changes significantly beyond expectations, market growth rates change significantly, or business performance becomes unpredictable, your board will want to understand the underlying reasons for the changes. Otherwise, they may conclude that your plan was not well thought out. Directors will also look for consistency of next year's operating plan with what you presented the previous July.

Your board will also be assessing current performance against the KPIs discussed in chapter 2 to make sure that the current operating plan and strategy is valid and being implemented successfully. Take the time to remind your board of current performance to establish additional credibility for your longer-term strategies. This knowledge can also be helpful when it comes time for your annual performance appraisal.

The board's final evaluation tool is a bit more intriguing and sometimes subtle. When you come to your board with acquisition candidates or other major investments that were not included in the plan, your board may ask a series of provocative questions. Is the acquisition or investment consistent with the strategy they approved? Why wasn't this investment part of your strategic plan? Why didn't you anticipate these investments in your plan? Was it because of poor planning, market changes, or some other reason? Think carefully about your strategic plan and how seriously you take it because these board questions can become increasingly difficult if there are major deviations in your strategy with no apparent cause.

Assessing Strategy Performance

Strategic planning is a key responsibility of every CEO and will be an important component of your annual performance appraisal. Long-term value creation is every CEO's mandate. The thoughtfulness and quality of your strategic plan—to meet customer needs and to provide the products and services they want—is the foundation for creating shareholder value.

Prudent market and competitive assessment, product roadmaps, investment, and developing your management team with the skills and experience to meet these needs on a sustained basis are all critical for success. Your board will assess your performance on each of these areas.

Summary

Your company's long-term strategic plan is one of the most important activities that you and your board undertake every year. The successful development and implementation of a well-considered long-term strategic plan can create significant shareholder value. A poorly considered plan can rapidly destroy value.

A board expects a disciplined, collaborative approach to strategy development, including the properly briefing board members and tapping into their experience. You can expect vigorous discussion of the planning assumptions, strategies, resource commitments, and the feasibility of successfully executing your proposed strategy.

Your board will use the strategy development process as an important indicator of CEO and management team performance. Effective strategy development is one of the major criteria the board uses in their annual evaluation of your performance.

Chapter Four
CEO Succession Planning

Succession planning for the CEO and other key senior management positions is one of the most important responsibilities for any CEO and his or her board of directors. Your board will expect you to take this responsibility seriously. They will likely devote the majority of time at one board meeting each year to review and discuss this topic.

The importance of CEO succession planning and management development is driven by the realization that successful companies are built on a foundation of strong and effective leadership. Technology and innovative products are important, but sustainable success comes from having the right people and management in place to meet customer needs and competitive demands. Today, the competition for talent has become fierce and is likely to remain so. Your board will expect that your ability to attract, assess, develop, and retain talent is one of your most important jobs.

As CEO, your board will depend on you to provide fact-based assessments of your senior managers and their potential to assume additional responsibility and possibly succeed you. Additionally, they will expect that your direct reports and other critical leadership positions have succession plans to ensure continuity of a strong management team. Help your board structure a process of continuous discussions about potential successors and the strength of your management team.

Plan Development and Approval Process

At all times, your board will expect that an immediate short-term succession plan be in place in the event that you are unable to perform your duties as CEO. This immediate succession plan does not necessarily need to be final; it can be an interim plan, covering up to six or nine months. If no internal candidate is ready to be CEO on a continuing basis, it is particularly important to have considered ongoing leadership in an emergency situation. This emergency plan provides the time for the board to conduct whatever internal and external searches are needed for a new CEO.

Many boards will expect your succession plan to be organized into three time horizons—immediate successor, ready in one to two years, and ready in three to five years. The immediate successor might not be the long-term successor but could adequately do the job in the short term to provide continuity of leadership and oversight until a permanent successor is found.

Effective CEO succession planning usually sets the tone for the people assessment and development process in the entire organization—not just the top management team. The succession planning and management development process is similar no matter the level of the organization. Acquiring entry-level talent and the continuous assessment and development of that talent pool is critical to the generation of new mid-level managers five to ten years from now. The assessment and development of current mid-level managers provides the feeder pool for your future senior executives. Finally, the assessment and development of your senior executives provides the feeder pool for your succession.

The assessment and development process begins with an honest discussion of each individual's performance, potential, and desire to assume additional responsibility. Gaming or short-circuiting this process and avoiding open and honest discussions achieves little. It is inexcusable for any CEO or senior executive to refuse to spend the time and effort required to do this process correctly.

Direct discussions with your executives, your personal observations, and possibly a 360-degree feedback assessment will provide very actionable information for assessing talent and developing plans for their personal development plan. The 360-degree assessment tool provides valuable input from the subordinate, peer, and supervisor perspectives. Standardization of this process provides annual input that can be compared over several years to track the leadership development progress for each of your senior executives.

These tools also provide objective information sources for you to review with your board so that directors gain a better appreciation for your leadership team, their strengths and weaknesses, and how they are developing as leaders.

As your direct reports see how you implement this process effectively, you will become their role model. They will then become the teachers and role models to their direct reports, and individual development plans will spread throughout the company. This process, when institutionalized, strengthens managerial bench strength reaching far down into the organization.

Monitoring CEO Succession Planning

Most boards formally devote one board meeting a year to CEO succession and management development discussions. During this meeting, you should present to your board, in executive session, your assessment of each individual of your management team, their strengths, weaknesses and development opportunities. The board needs your honest assessment of their potential to replace you. If they truly are potential CEO succession candidates, two questions need to be answered: What additional personal development must be completed for you to recommend them as your successor? What are your plans to develop these needed skills and experience?

Some boards may also expect some of your direct reports in key roles to present succession plans for their positions, including the top two to three people in their respective organizations following the same format. This provides the board with an opportunity to evaluate each executive's capability to assess and develop his or her direct reports.

Assessing Your Performance

A strong succession-planning process and management assessment and development process both require strong top-down CEO leadership. You are directly accountable for the quality of your succession plan, evaluation of candidates, and development progress made with each individual identified as a potential successor. Expect your board to use the quality of the process you implement and the development of your leadership team and potential successors as a key determinant of your performance as CEO. If there is no immediate successor ready to replace you, the board will expect you to begin to identify and develop internal candidates or hire suitable external candidates who have the potential to be your successor. The continued lack of potential succession candidates for your position or some of your key management positions will be deemed unacceptable by your board.

The board needs to spend time with the most promising internal succession candidates. Directors must form their own opinions of their capabilities, business acumen, strengths and weaknesses, and leadership styles. The board will want to assess the way your organization responds to each candidate. Board presentations offer one view but are usually structured and sometimes rehearsed so the true performance and potential of a candidate may not be apparent. Directors need to spend quality time with potential candidates in different settings to develop valid assessments.

As CEO, you should expect your own annual performance assessment will be based on specific performance criteria on which you and your board jointly agree at the start of each year. The evaluation will be based on both objective and subjective criteria. The principal criteria will include business performance versus approved plan, accomplishment of long-term strategic objectives, CEO succession planning, and management development. Additionally, the board may assess your performance in more subjective areas such as adherence to company values, leadership style, and your ability to assess, develop, and retain talent. Each board will have its own process to discuss and agree upon the specific performance criteria against which you'll be evaluated. Your annual performance assessment should not be a surprise. Throughout the year, work with your lead director, if you have one, or one of the most respected directors to gather feedback on your performance. Your personal performance evaluation will form the basis of the compensation committee's discussions about considering and recommending your compensation to the full board for approval.

Summary

CEO succession planning is an important board responsibility and ultimately one of the most important board decisions they will make. Your board will actively seek and value your input in the process and should continually provide feedback to you. It is important for you to maintain frequent and candid dialogue with your board on this topic.

A strong and sustainable management succession plan is built on what your company needs in terms of skills, experience, and leadership. Your business strategy and the current operating results determine these needs. Thus, management development and succession planning becomes the third leg of the stool. It's the reason why good CEOs devote so much time to working on this topic and discussing it with their boards. It also ties the people and leadership requirements together to successfully implement your annual operating plan and longer term strategy.

One of your most important responsibilities is to ensure that you have a diverse and deep management team in place now and developing the talent pool to achieve future growth. Much has been said and written about the war for talent. To win this war for talent, your entire senior management team must be focused on assessing, developing, and retaining outstanding talent. This begins at the top with strong leadership from you and needs to permeate your entire organization.

Chapter Five
Risk Management

Over the past several years, boards have increasingly focused on the area of risk management. These risks go well beyond the financial reporting risks that the Sarbanes-Oxley Act was designed to minimize. When risk is discussed, many times the immediate assumption and reaction can be that it's focused primarily on compliance to regulations like Sarbanes-Oxley. Are the controls in place? Are they being adhered to? Are the risks material?

Initially, audit committees evaluated financial controls to ensure regulatory compliance and the reliability and integrity of financial reporting. Risk discussions have expanded to include the guidelines and policies that govern the process by which the company's exposure to risk is assessed and managed. These key business risk areas are described in your company's 10-K and 10-Q filings. Boards now want to proactively understand the magnitude and probability of these risks, which risks are within your control, and what risk mitigation plans are in place. It is likely that in the foreseeable future, more stringent guidelines will be enacted to define how boards should deal with risk oversight.

No Risk, No Reward

Risk is an inherent part of every business. The old adage "no risk, no reward" is truer today than ever. So if risk can't be eliminated, how can it be mitigated and adequately managed? That's the area on which boards will increasingly focus—the identification and mitigation of prudent risk. It will become part of your business reviews, strategy discussions, audit committee meetings, and it will be interwoven into many other board discussions. Your board will insist that you and your team undertake a process of systematic identification and management of business risks in your strategy and all business activities.

Every business risk can have positive or negative outcomes. Successfully managed risk can be the source of significant competitive advantage. Poorly managed risk can create a competitive disadvantage and a distraction from other business activities.

If risk is continually mismanaged with negative consequences, it's easy to fall into a trap of risk avoidance, which can rapidly lead to mediocrity and loss of competitive position. Poor management of risk detracts from shareholder value and can be costly.

How Well Do You Understand Your Business Risks?

Your board will be assessing the ability of your management team to objectively understand the business risks you are facing. Are your risks prudent with a good balance of potential gain and loss? Have you planned wisely to avoid assuming too much uncontrollable risk? Do your plans minimize risks through viable contingency plans put in place before the risk is assumed? Does your management learn from risks and the resulting outcomes? Are your compensation plans encouraging too much risk?

In short, you and your management team will need to continually demonstrate that your plans and strategies adequately assess and manage the financial and business performance risks that you assumed in your annual operating plan and long-term strategy.

Prioritize Your Risks

Specifically, each major risk should be clearly defined and then prioritized. Criteria for prioritizing include the relative impact on your business, the likelihood of occurrence, and finally how much control you have over each risk. For the prioritized list, mitigation plans should be developed for each risk with clear responsibilities and ownership. These risks and mitigation plans should be reviewed at least annually with your board. Critically important risks may require special reviews with the board during normal quarterly board meetings.

Effective risk management will become increasingly essential for good business performance and value creation. Effectively managed, risk becomes a competitive advantage to which competitors will not be able to readily react. As CEO, you need to establish a culture of prudent risk taking and effective risk management. There must be clear executive ownership and continuous support for the importance of the risk management process. Your board will be carefully observing and assessing your level of risk tolerance and judgment reflected in your annual operating plan, long-term strategy, and assessment and development of senior talent. Over time, your board will have ample data points to evaluate and assess this important area. From their own experience, your directors should be able to provide valuable counsel and perspective from lessons they've learned the hard way.

CEO Leadership Is Required

One of the most important aspects of effective risk management is your top-down leadership. You will need to establish and nurture a culture that accepts and manages prudent risk. This is a difficult leadership challenge, but it must permeate all levels of the organization. We are all familiar with risk-averse companies that have a culture of everyone keeping their head down, so they won't get shot. In these companies, failure has clear consequences, but success often goes unrewarded. Increasingly, decisions are postponed or never made because more data and more clarity are needed before the risk can be assumed. In today's fast-moving competitive world, this type of risk-avoidance culture is ineffective and will not be acceptable to your board.

Effective risk management creates an environment that invigorates employees, challenges them to perform better, and makes work rewarding.

This type of corporate culture can help you attract and retain the best talent. Great people are the key differentiator between the best companies and mediocre ones. Decisions are made faster, more effectively, and with less effort. The risks are not assumed haphazardly but are imbedded in a robust yet fast analytical planning process that is a model for all processes in the company. In many ways, effective risk management is a leading indicator of future corporate performance.

Successful risk management integrates operational, strategic, financial, and compliance components into a well-honed managerial discipline. It is palpable and immediately visible to all. Conversely, poor risk management is a weight that pulls down the entire organization. Decisions become overly complex, slow, and cumbersome. This is a recipe for poor performance.

The process for effective risk management needs to be deeply imbedded in the fabric of the company. There needs to be a clear and integrated link between the strategy, operational plans, and staffing, skills, and people development.

Successful CEOs take a proactive role in framing the subject of risk management and reporting to their boards. Your leadership on this issue can prioritize board discussions and provide your directors with a sense of confidence that you and your team understand the importance of this issue and are assuming and managing prudent risks to create shareholder value.

Summary

Effective risk management can reduce costs and improve business performance. Both of these positive results will create value for your shareholders and potentially sustainable competitive advantage. When risks are properly identified and effectively managed, you and your board members can focus far more time and energy on growth strategies and creating value for your shareholders.

As you and your board focus more time on risk management, expect that the board may view this topic differently from you and your management team. Because much of your focus will be on operational issues that can affect the business today, you may become frustrated as your board starts to discuss and ask questions about long-term and higher-level risks. While this may be frustrating, please keep in mind that your directors will be bringing their perspective and lessons learned from personal experience with risk to these discussions. I encourage you to take the time to learn from their experiences and insights.

Chapter Six
Audit Committee

Working effectively with board committees is another important component for successfully managing your relationship with your board. The committees are composed of only a few directors and tend to focus on specific topics. This affords you the opportunity to forge a closer working relationship with your directors.

Typical Board Committees

All boards have a minimum of three standing committees to assist in providing strong governance. These are the audit, compensation, and nominating and governance committees. The audit committee oversees the financial reporting practices and the company's relationship with their independent auditor. The compensation committee recommends CEO and senior management compensation to the full board and oversees your company's compensations plans and programs. The nominating and governance committee oversees corporate governance, conducts the annual board evaluation and recommends candidates to fill board vacancies.

Independent directors are usually chosen to serve on these committees based on their skills and experience to ensure that each committee meets all legal and regulatory requirements.

Depending on a company's specific needs, boards may have established other committees to improve governance or to play a key advisory role to the full board. Some examples include a finance committee, strategic planning committee, risk management committee, social and corporate responsibility committee, or a technology committee. The overarching strategies for you to work effectively with the audit, compensation, and nominating and governance committees also apply to these special committees, if they are in place on your board.

Sometimes, important issues arise and the board may form a special committee to deal with it. Examples include evaluating acquisitions; internal investigations; corporate responsibility issues; and policies on legislative, regulatory, or judicial matters. Special committees can also be useful when there is a potential conflict of interest or when the board's decision-making process might not be totally independent. This can occur because of the real or perceived conflicts of interests with one or more directors. Assignments to these special committees are usually driven by the expertise of the directors and their availability to devote the necessary time. This has proven to be an excellent and efficient use of board resources.

In the following sections, I'll discuss each of the three core committees in more detail and provide some additional perspective on their focus and priorities. There are common threads on the CEO's role and involvement, not only on these three committees but also on others the board may establish. Successful CEOs realize the importance of attending as many committee meetings as their schedules permit. The insights these meetings provide are well worth the time. Naturally, each committee will have an executive session that excludes management, but that's a small part of committee discussions. To be an effective CEO, you need to know firsthand the issues on which each committee is focused, and you must ensure that you and your management team are addressing them.

Audit Committee Functions

The audit committee is responsible for overseeing the accounting and financial reporting processes of your company, audits of your financial statements, and the internal controls over your financial processes. All members of your audit committee will be independent directors as required by listing exchanges and regulatory requirements. At least one member must be a certified financial expert. All committee members should be financially literate and well-versed in business, financial, and accounting matters. Each member must be able to read and understand fundamental financial statements and be knowledgeable about financial disclosure requirements.

The audit committee performs five fundamental functions:

1. Oversee the independent auditor's qualifications and independence.
2. Assess and ensure adequate performance of the company's independent auditors.
3. Oversee the quality and integrity of the company's financial statements and related disclosures.
4. Ensure the adequacy of the systems of financial and IT internal control.
5. Oversee the scope and performance of the internal audit function.

Audit Committee Process

The audit committee needs a carefully designed meeting schedule to ensure that it discharges its fiduciary duties. As part of this schedule, the committee will meet quarterly with management, the independent auditor, and the director of internal audit to review financial results before each quarterly earnings release. The committee should also review the quarterly earnings press release and any proposed management guidance to investors.

Before commencing the annual audit, the committee reviews the proposed overall audit plan with the independent auditor and the members of management who are responsible for preparing the company's financial statements. The committee reviews and approves the scope and staffing of the independent auditor's annual audit plan. It is important that key members of your finance team attend committee discussions, including your chief financial officer, finance director, controller, director of tax, and director of internal audit.

At the quarterly committee meetings, management and the external auditor present issues to the committee that may significantly affect the reporting of your financial results. Additionally, any significant written communications or issues that have been discussed between management and the external auditors are reviewed with the committee. These include the management letter, internal control deficiencies, application of accounting principles, and off-balance sheet transactions. The committee is advised of the viewpoints on each issue and any disagreements between management and the external auditors on how the issue should be addressed. The audit committee is directly responsible for the resolution of disagreements between management and the independent auditor regarding financial reporting.

During its review, the audit committee discusses with the independent auditor any audit problems or significant reporting issues and management's response to these issues. This review includes any difficulties encountered by the auditor in the course of performing their audit work. These difficulties might include any restrictions on the scope of the auditor's activities or access to information and any significant disagreements with management. These discussions will occur first with management present, so management can respond and the committee can hear from both parties. It is then critical that the audit committee convene an executive session, without management present, so that the audit partner and key members of the audit team can speak freely without interference by management.

Most audit committees are not composed of board members who are professional accountants and auditors. Their role is to provide financial reporting oversight for the board and to provide advice, counsel, and direction to management and the external auditors.

Financial misstatements and, even worse, fraud, carry serious consequences for all involved. Aspersions and suspicion placed on management hinders their ability to perform at a high level. The board can be perceived to have unsatisfactorily exercised effective oversight, and the external auditors' credibility and financial judgment might be questioned. Finally, any financial irregularities in today's environment carry severe consequences for shareholders. It is not uncommon to see companies who fail to file their financial reports on time or need to restate financials penalized by losing 10 to 30 percent of their value. Some companies have lost more than 50 percent of their market capitalization.

The consequences of poor execution in the financial reporting area are quite serious, apart from falling short of legal and regulatory requirements. Audit committee members therefore take their responsibility very seriously and devote considerable time to their responsibilities. They expect that management will also continue to take financial reporting seriously also. Many audit committee charters state that the committee will meet at least four times a year, but almost all audit committees meet more frequently.

Working with Your Audit Committee

Boards and their audit committees have high expectations that can be summed up simply and clearly: any material inaccuracy in your financial filings, failure to meet regulatory requirements, or failure to file required financial reports on time is unacceptable and will not be tolerated by your board. The consequences for failure can be serious and swift.

Because of the gravity of its responsibility, the committee sometimes gets into exacting detail in their reviews. When the Sarbanes-Oxley Act (SOX) requirements were first enacted in 2002, most committees conducted extensive compliance reviews to ensure that management could demonstrate adequate documentation for all financial and IT controls. They also spent considerable time probing and evaluating management's control processes and investigating whether sufficient resources were being deployed to achieve SOX compliance. Some CEOs and their management teams were not entirely happy with this intrusion into their operation, but boards needed to be comfortable that SOX requirements would be met.

This points to a truism that permeates all parts of this book: When there is increased risk to your performance, achievement of your business objectives, or adherence to regulatory requirements, your board will take the required time and effort to get deeply involved in operational details so they can be assured that their management is doing the right thing. Some CEOs may perceive this as the board distrusting management or micromanaging. Today's boards view it as carrying out their responsibilities to the shareholders who elected them as directors.

As companies have satisfied their boards that the proper controls were in place to comply with SOX requirements, the focus has changed to ensuring compliance with all approved controls. Committee attention has shifted to identifying and understanding noncompliance incidences and trying to determine if there was a pattern that might indicate a more widespread execution problem.

Misrepresentation Starts Slowly

Most companies have an honest management team with high integrity. Relatively few companies have experienced outright fraud and deceit for personal gain, best characterized by lying, cheating, and stealing.

From a financial misstatement and fraud standpoint, directors are acutely aware that most issues occur slowly over time and many are not even initiated maliciously. They usually occur because there is a shortfall in revenues or earnings, so actions are taken on a relatively small scale to make the quarter and the expectations held by investors. Those committing the misstatements believe that they can reverse their actions next quarter, when things get better. Regretfully, the next quarter usually doesn't get better, and the misstatement gets bigger eventually progressing to the point of major fraud.

Potential Areas for Misrepresentation

From a practical standpoint, these undesirable activities will most likely occur in two discrete areas: revenue recognition and expense accounting. Expect your audit committee to spend significant time on both of these areas. Committee reviews can probe deeply into the timing and amounts of any revenue estimates based on percentage of project completion and complex transactions, how reserves are set and used, and the timing of accounting for expenses.

As CEO, it is very important that you take the time to attend audit committee meetings. You will see firsthand what are the important issues and concerns of your directors. You will also be able to evaluate the strength of your finance team in providing answers to directors' questions. Sometimes, these committee meetings may feel like an inquisition as the board members pepper your team with questions. Sometimes, they ask questions from multiple perspectives as crosschecks. It may seem that the directors don't trust you, your CFO, or your team. You might become defensive because it appears that directors are on a witch- hunt to find discrepancies. Sometimes, you may conclude that the directors are simply trying to legally protect themselves as board members.

Nothing could be further from the truth. Committee members are fulfilling their fiduciary responsibilities. Many have been on your side of the table as CEOs. They have managed businesses, had to make their quarterly numbers, and have been asked questions by their own boards and audit committees. Good directors will always be respectful, but expect the questions to continue. If they begin to see any issues that concern them, expect the questioning and probing to rapidly intensify.

Use Internal Audit as a Resource

The internal audit function is responsible for independently reviewing and evaluating the adequacy, effectiveness, and quality of your internal controls related to your financial statements and assets. This function provides an independent and objective assessment of the adequacy and effectiveness of your internal control environment.

Internal audit provides a systematic, disciplined approach to evaluating and improving the effectiveness of controls and risk management for the entire business. Based on an annual internal audit plan that the audit committee reviews and approves, internal audit prepares reports with analyses and recommendations. It also reviews and assesses management's response to the audit findings and recommendations.

The audit committee has charged the internal audit function to systematically evaluate and recommend improvements for increasing the effectiveness of risk management and business processes. This enables management to be more effective in meeting its business objectives. Initial activities focused on reviewing and evaluating the company's financial reporting controls to satisfy SOX requirements. This has been and will remain an important component of this function. The development and execution of an annual internal audit plan that prioritizes activities and resources on the basis of greatest potential risk is growing in importance.

When internal audit completes an audit, the preliminary findings and recommendations are normally discussed with management responsible for the area reviewed. Your responses and action plans to recommendations will be incorporated into a final audit report distributed to the audit committee, senior management, and the company's external auditors. Follow-up on management action plans will be performed and reported at audit committee meetings. Good CEOs take an active role ensuring that the management response to issues identified by internal audit rapidly resolve any deficiencies.

Summary

The audit committee's responsibility is one of oversight on behalf of the board of directors. It is the responsibility of management to establish and maintain appropriate systems of financial record keeping and internal controls, to report exceptions to such controls to the committee, and to prepare consolidated financial statements in accordance with the applicable financial standards. It is the responsibility of the company's independent auditor to audit those financial statements prepared by management. Each member of the committee relies on the accuracy and integrity of those persons and organizations within and outside the company from whom he or she receives information.

Attending audit committee meetings provides you with many important perspectives. First, you get a better understanding of the financial issues and controls that are important to your directors. Second, you get to see your finance team in action, interacting with board members. Finally, you get the opportunity to develop closer and more personal relationships with individual directors. The investment of your time to attend these committee meetings will pay great dividends in your ability to effectively work with your board.

Chapter Seven
Compensation Committee

The compensation committee is responsible for reviewing and approving executive compensation policies and programs consistent with corporate objectives and shareholder interests. All members of the compensation committee are independent directors.

Compensation committees perform four key functions:

1. Review and approve the company's compensation philosophy and its implementation.
2. Approve specific compensation awards for executive officers, including cash bonuses, equity grants, retirement and severance compensation packages, as well as bonus pools for all employees and significant changes to compensation and benefit plans.
3. Review and recommend for full board approval director and CEO compensation.
4. Review and approve the compensation discussion and analysis (CD&A) section of proxy to conform to SEC disclosure requirements.

Compensation Committee Process

The fundamental role of the committee is to ensure that compensation practices yield the expected business results. Decisions are made in the context of competitive compensation practices by a peer group of companies. The committee determines the appropriate peer group and performance measures for executive compensation. Independent compensation consultants are used as needed to support committee tasks.

Each year, the committee will review the design and effectiveness of your annual and long-term incentive compensation programs. The committee's charge is to ensure that your compensation plans are properly aligned with and support your business strategy, are fair and equitable, and will create value for your shareholders. The context of this review is based on the long-term strategy and annual operating plans that have been developed by management and approved by the board.

One of the most important functions of the compensation committee is to prepare a recommendation to the full board on the compensation, policies, and programs for you and your executive officers. The committee must ensure that all senior executive compensation programs are aligned with the business strategy and the short-term and long-term interests of your shareholders. The committee's review should be supported by a fact-based analysis to ensure that the executive compensation plan attracts, retains, and motivates executives to be successful in your business environment and enhances shareholder value without incurring unnecessary risk.

The committee is also responsible for reviewing and approving the annual CD&A report that is now an important component of each annual proxy statement. In addition to verifying that the company has met all regulatory disclosure requirements clearly and accurately, the committee should identify compensation issues that the full board will need to address in the coming year.

Compensation Philosophy

Your company's philosophy and approach to employee and executive compensation needs to balance the realities of the marketplace while increasing shareholder value in a cost efficient manner. It must also balance shareholder value creation over the short-term and a longer-term time horizon.

Boards are increasingly focused on the principle of pay for performance balanced with the need to attract and retain senior management talent in a fiercely competitive market environment. To strike the proper balance, directors need to understand the most important drivers of shareholder value creation and reward management for performance against these drivers. Stretch but attainable performance goals need to be established that are consistent with the approved annual operating plan and long-term business strategy. Finally, the committee needs to be sure that all compensation and incentive plans will reward the desired behavior as well as results.

This is no easy task. Throughout their careers, many directors and CEOs have personally designed and implemented compensation plans that they sincerely thought would achieve their objectives only to find that there were unintended consequences. With the proper process and review mechanisms, you and your board can make corrections as needed. In an ever-changing business environment, you need to strive to strike a delicate balance between reward and motivation for your senior executives, while maintaining a competitive compensation position. The compensation plan must also be acceptable to your shareholders and not cause management to take excessive risk.

Compensation as a Lead Indicator

A strong board will view executive compensation and the process used to determine it as a lead indicator of board performance and the relationship the board has with their CEO. Poor performance in this area indicates that there may be issues between the board and its CEO or serious governance issues. This point is very important, so let me take a moment to demonstrate the linkage between good compensation practices and broader governance practices encompassing operational governance, strategic planning, and succession planning and management development.

At a high level, compensation for you and your executive officers is composed of a base salary, a bonus given in cash or equity, and long-term retention equity. I'll exclude employee benefits, perquisites, and other smaller compensation programs from this discussion. I'll also assume that your base salary is consistent with salaries at comparable companies.

To properly determine annual salary increases, a robust annual performance assessment needs to be performed for you and each of your executive officers. To complete this assessment, there needs to be clear performance objectives and measurements resulting in an assessment of actual performance versus objectives. Salary increases are not given arbitrarily but are based on the level of performance achieved. Annual incentives, either equity or cash, are also based on performance. Thus the annual assessment process drives effective execution of pay for performance.

To determine long-term equity awards, three components are required. First is an assessment of the potential for each executive. How much more responsibility or growth potential do they have? Secondly, what is the long-term growth strategy for your company and what are the skill and experience requirements to successfully implement that strategy? Finally, how does the current performance and growth potential of the individual fit into your long-term strategy? Those executives who perform, are a good fit, and have higher potential deserve superior equity awards to retain and motivate this important talent pool.

The drivers of structure of the compensation philosophy and plan are clearly the three key areas of board focus: operational performance, strategy, and succession planning. The equity and financial rewards are predicated on successful achievement of objectives for operational performance, business strategy, and management development. It easy to see how executive compensation is truly a lead indicator of CEO and board performance, and the quality of the relationship between the two. It is a critical link between performance, potential, and the processes used to run your company.

From a CEO and board interaction perspective, if the compensation process appears to be failing, some very serious questions need to be answered:

1. Is management's compensation philosophy and high-level compensation plan fundamentally flawed?
2. Has management set the correct performance objectives and are they measurable?
3. Does management have a clear and actionable long-term strategic plan?

4. Does management implement an effective annual performance appraisal process?
5. Does management implement an effective process to assess and develop talent?
6. Does the board have the correct governance processes and self-assessment tools in place?

Working with your Compensation Committee

As CEO, you are responsible for each of these areas. Your board provides support, counsel, and oversight. Thus, when a problem is noted with executive officer compensation, you and the board need to immediately assess whether more fundamental issues need to be addressed.

Since compensation is a leading indicator of your relationship and interaction with your board, let's take a moment to bring this higher level, impartial approach down to the personal level and discuss the process for your performance assessment and compensation determination.

Early each year, you and the board should agree on a series of specific performance objectives that you are expected to achieve consistent with the approved annual operating plan. Some of your performance objectives also are critical to achieving the approved long-term strategic plan.

At year-end, the directors will conduct your annual performance appraisal. Some boards use the nonexecutive chair or lead director to facilitate independent director discussions to crystallize the board's assessment of your performance. You should provide the board with your own input in the form of a self-assessment. You should carefully review the board's assessment and discuss any differences. When you reach agreement on your performance assessment, the compensation committee will prepare a recommendation for full board approval for your compensation, including base salary, annual incentives, and long-term equity incentive awards.

For your direct reports, you should follow the same process: prepare their performance assessments, obtain their own self-assessments, obtain peer feedback, and obtain feedback from relevant direct reports. Then prepare your overall assessment and recommendation to the compensation committee.

The process the board uses to determine your compensation is the template you should use for your management team and, in fact, the entire organization. If you and your board lack a good process to evaluate your performance and determine compensation, you should expect to see similar deficiencies in the company's overall compensation process. Compensation really is a leading indicator of board governance and management performance.

For a compensation committee to effectively and efficiently perform its responsibilities and to help make the best possible decisions, they need you and your executive team to play an active role in compensation input and design. Only you and your team are close enough to your employees to truly understand what motivates them and provides value while being cost effective for your shareholders. This is critical input that only you and your team can provide since everyone is motivated differently. Additionally, you and your team are closest to the market and competitive dynamics that play a major role in determining the amount and construct of incentive programs.

Support Resources

In addition to your personal involvement, your vice president of human resources, director of compensation, and your CFO are important support resources for the committee. As senior leadership of the company, you are all well-versed in employee compensation issues as well as the competitive environment to successfully attract and retain good employees.

You and the vice president of human resources are the key drivers of the performance appraisal process and leadership development. You both lead the process to assess the senior talent pool in terms of performance and potential, which are important determinants of executive compensation in terms of salary, cash incentives, and equity that can provide valuable employee retention value.

Summary

Shareholders, angry at what they perceive to be excessive executive compensation, have placed increased pressure on all compensation committees to better align executive compensation with shareholder interests. In response, committees have begun a process to review current compensation plans and will adjust compensation plans if necessary to ensure consistency with creation of shareholder value. In the process, directors will continuously probe and question areas that in the past were the province of the CEO. Recommendations you may have made in the past that were approved with minimal discussion now require much more discussion and debate. Committees will require fact-based compensation comparisons and will use their own independent compensation advisers to determine the best executive compensation packages to achieve business objectives.

If a compensation committee fails to fulfill its responsibility, they can expect investors to become more aggressive and demanding. Investors may either mount an effort to place their own directors on the board or send the board a clear message of dissatisfaction by withholding votes for directors.

Chapter Eight
Nominating and Governance Committee

The role of the nominating and governance committee (N&G) is to ensure the proper governance of a company. The committee is responsible for discussing and recommending the appropriate size, functions, and needs of the board to ensure effective governance. Specifically, this means two things: (1) that there is a diverse group of independent directors with the correct skill sets and experiences and (2) that there are the proper governance processes to fulfill board fiduciary responsibilities and create value for your shareholders.

The functions of the committee can be categorized into two main areas: director selection and governance process.

1. Director Selection
The committee identifies and recommends director nominees to ensure that the board and its committees are staffed with the requisite expertise and experience to create shareholder value, provide good governance, and provide guidance to the CEO.

2. Governance Process
The committee ensures that board governance process meets all regulatory requirements and provides adequate oversight for shareholders. This includes conducting an annual review of board performance and governance processes, and providing opportunities for board members to maintain

proficiency in business and governance issues so they can exercise their responsibilities.

Nominating and Governance Committee Process

The N&G committee's responsibilities have evolved considerably as boards have become increasingly independent. Much of the overall success of a board is dependent upon an effectively functioning N&G committee. Let's look deeper into each of the two main areas of responsibility and consider how a CEO can work effectively with this committee.

Director Selection and Nomination

A primary role of the committee is to identify candidates who are qualified to be directors of your company. This includes identifying and interviewing potential directors, as well as evaluating and recommending existing directors who are standing for reelection. The committee is charged with recommending a slate of nominees to the full board for consideration and approval. When approved, these nominees are proposed for election by the shareholders at their annual meeting.

When the committee reviews the skills and characteristics of board members, they will pay specific attention to professional experience and position, character, commitment to serve, and diversity of background. Each of these characteristics needs to be placed in the context of the requirements of your board at that time. For existing directors who are renominated, the committee needs to carefully evaluate past attendance at board meetings, the director's quality of participation in board activities, and the contribution he or she made during the last term.

Strong nominating and governance committees periodically assess the skill requirements needed to meet changing business requirements. Then the committee is in a better position to nominate directors who provide the needed skills while pruning directors whose skills are no longer valuable.

As CEO, you must actively participate in these discussions and make sure that your point of view is presented clearly. This applies to both identifying potential new directors as well as providing feedback on existing directors who are standing for reelection.

Governance Process

The committee needs to monitor significant developments in corporate governance and changes in the responsibilities of directors and lead the board in its annual self-appraisal. It oversees compliance with your company's code of business ethics, and develops and recommends governance guidelines for the full board to discuss and approve.

The committee leads the discussion process on new and evolving board governance issues. As has been noted earlier, the governance of corporations today is continually evolving because of legislative, regulatory, or shareholder activities. This committee must be the repository of the knowledge of these changes and their effect on your company. Additionally, they must carefully evaluate and discuss which optional governance changes are beneficial to the company and which changes should be avoided. They must conduct this evaluation objectively and avoid being pressured by external forces to do things that are not in the best interests of the company.

Again, it is important that you are aware of the issues under consideration, participate in the discussions, and voice your point of view. Some of the potential governance changes may not provide value to you and the company or may increase workload with minimal benefit. Your directors need to understand your opinion and thought process before they make a final determination on changes in their corporate governance.

It's important that every board evaluate their own performance and relationship with their CEO annually. The governance committee is charged with leading this evaluation, compiling the results, and reviewing them with the full board and the CEO. The committee should also prepare proposals for improving the governance process where opportunities exist. These opportunities can include changes in board meeting agendas and focus, meeting frequency and duration, committee structures and assignments, and any other areas that will improve governance.

Your Input Is Invaluable

It's important that you find a way to share your thoughts on governance process and issues, as well as director selection. Are individual directors being helpful and responsive when you seek advice? Are any directors causing problems for you or the management team by interfering in business operations? What could the board be doing that would help you and your team be more successful? Answers to these questions can be discussed in executive sessions of the board, or in sensitive matters, through the help of the lead director.

It's important that you spend time with the nominating and governance committee identifying the skill sets and experience necessary for directors to properly govern your company and provide relevant counsel to you and the management team. It is also important that you actively participate in the identification of the required director skill sets and provide input into the selection and nomination of directors.

You need to work with your board to attract the proper mix of directors who can meet present and future business challenges. Based on meeting agenda topics, it's important that you periodically identify the board skills and experience required to help guide the company for sustainable growth. Your perspective on these requirements is important if you are to have an effective board. However, to maintain independence, final nomination of directors must be approved by a majority of independent directors.

It is important that the board receive your input and feedback on their performance. The ideal time to discuss any issues or observations is immediately after each board meeting. Ideally, you and the board should have a feedback process; either through the lead director or another designated director.

Orientation for New Directors

Make yourself and your management team available to new directors so that he or she is well-versed on your business and the major issues you are facing. The more a director understands your business, the more value he or she can provide to you, your team, and the board.

As new directors are elected to the board, you need to ensure that there is a proper orientation process. This orientation includes meetings with you and members of senior management, so the new director is familiar with current business performance, strategic plans, competition, technology, significant financial accounting, and risk management issues. The new director should meet with the independent auditor as well as your director of internal audit. The nominating and governance committee should provide background on board governance processes, committee assignments, corporate code of conduct and expectations for board members.

Summary

In the past, many CEOs selected new board members and the board's role was more of a chemistry check to ensure the new members would work well with existing members. As the governance pendulum has swung toward more independence, the selection process for new and existing directors has changed. The CEO now provides input to the N&G committee and the full board, but the decision is solely a board decision. In fact, the final question in some cases now becomes, can the CEO effectively work with the new director? Obviously, either case, carried to extreme, is potentially detrimental to governance of the business as well as support to you as CEO. The ideal approach is to jointly identify and vet candidates, realizing that only the board nominates and shareholders vote.

The committee also needs to carefully consider the feedback gained from the annual board evaluation. There should be structured discussions that include the CEO to determine opportunities for improvement in board processes. Your input and participation is important because any changes will directly affect you and your team. Proper corporate governance starts with the right set of directors who implement the best possible governance process. Well-considered, consistently implemented processes are the foundation of effective board functioning.

PART TWO:

DEVELOPING A SUCCESSFUL PLAN

Chapter Nine
Creating Your Plan

Once you have a broad understanding of the priorities and focus of your board and its committees, begin thinking about how to manage your interactions with the board so that you are both successful. Take some time now to craft a clear vision of how you want to work with the board. To start the process, think about how you would describe a successful relationship with the board twelve months from now. You can use questions about each of the five fundamental principles listed in the introduction as the starting point for what you want to achieve. Appendix 2 contains additional questions on each principle for deeper reflection.

1. Understand your board's focus and expectations

Chapters 1 through 8 described the focus, governance implications, expectations, and importance of the entire board, as well as each committee. List your understanding of the priorities for your board and for each of the board committees. How will you periodically verify this information for your board and ensure that your understanding is always current?

2. Provide timely, accurate, and relevant information to your directors

The information resources available to your board are critical to effective governance as well as providing the most help to make you successful. How will you ensure that the content, frequency, and format of information continuously meet board needs?

3. Establish effective two-way communication with your board and individual directors.

The chemistry and interaction between you and the board needs to be open, honest, and candid. How will you ensure that your interactions with the board and individual directors are conducive to meaningful participation and open two-way dialogue?

4. Develop a robust, continual personal assessment and feedback process

Knowing how the board views your performance, their level of satisfaction with the information they receive, and quality of their interaction with you are all vital to a successful long-term relationship. What processes and techniques will you use to get timely and actionable feedback from your board?

5. Use continual change as an opportunity to enhance your board relationship

The only thing that is certain is change. How will you stay abreast of new governance issues, changing expectations, and evolving interpersonal dynamics so you are responsive to the needs of your board?

There are no simplistic answers to these questions. You will probably find that the answers change over time. These five questions can help you reflect and organize ideas that will continuously shape your relationship with the board. You can periodically revisit these questions to identify new opportunities to strengthen your board interactions.

The balance of this book deals with proven tactics that support achievement of each of these fundamental principles. Extract from each section the ideas that you think will work best for you based on your style and knowledge of your board and individual directors. Your objective should not be to create the perfect plan. Start doing the right things now and correct your course based on the feedback you receive.

Importance of Your Initial Board Meetings

Navigating the crucial and complex relationship with your board is a hallmark of a successful CEO. It's important to get off to a fast start. Ideally, this begins day one as a CEO, but even if you have been in the job for a while, it's never too late to start implementing many of these ideas. Learning to work successfully with your board during your first year can be very important because it creates a strong foundation for success in the future.

If you have been CEO for a while, you may have to work harder to improve your working relationship with your board—particularly if tensions have developed. I'll discuss some of the common tensions that can develop between a CEO and board in chapter 10. However, if you have issues with your board or individual directors, don't give up. There is always an opportunity to establish a better relationship with your board, but you have to take the leadership role and actively manage the process.

Get the Fundamentals Right

Building a successful relationship with your board is built on very simple but critical fundamental behaviors, skills, and processes. These may seem obvious to you, but poor execution of the basics is the downfall of many an executive. Execution of these fundamentals between you and the board are no exception. You cannot assume that just because you are all accomplished and successful executives, the fundamentals will be executed well.

As board workload continues to increase, agendas and time management become increasingly important. Also, the quality and timing of briefing materials distributed to the board have become more critical. Committees are meeting longer and more frequently. More information is prepared for the board members to review and digest. Directors need to devote more time to learning and maintaining current knowledge of the business and board issues. Increased workloads for directors cause increased workloads for CEOs. This means that all communication and every interaction must be carefully focused and succinct to meet the needs of directors.

Combining All the Pieces into an Effective Working Relationship

The foundations for an effective relationship with your board begin with implementing the fundamentals of good meeting organization and planning. These start with a clear focus and set of priorities for the board and its committees. Board calendars, agendas, and meeting materials are then structured and organized according to these priorities to achieve the desired governance results and the optimal level of support for you. While this may all seem obvious, each of us has experienced meetings when a lack of focus, poor calendar planning, lack of a clear agenda, or insufficient information significantly diminished the meeting's value.

The starting point for board materials is the content and quantity of material needed by the board and its committees to exercise their fiduciary and decision-making responsibilities. Some directors will have a personal preference for receiving the information, and some may have special information requests. The needs of the board, not management convenience, drive all of these support requirements. As in many things in business, success is achieved because attention is paid to the details.

Board Calendar

The annual board calendar is the structural basis of successful governance. The calendar needs to include full board meetings integrated with committee agendas and meetings. Clear deliverables and priorities need to be set for each committee and the board. A well-considered calendar ensures that the board carries out its legal and fiduciary responsibilities and that it discusses the correct business issues. This provides a working structure that will provide the most value to you because it helps define clear information requirements.

The increased volume and complexity of board work requires you and the board to continually evaluate and refine board and committee meeting schedules, and the amount of time devoted to each meeting and to important topics.

Board Agendas

In recent years, board meeting and committee agendas have evolved to reflect the changing relative importance of issues, decisions that needed to be made, and time for the board to discuss major topics. The most successful board meetings share two components: first, a major discussion topic based on one of the four board priorities covered in chapters 2-5: annual operating plan, strategic plan, CEO succession planning, and risk management. Second are the important subject areas is discussed in the next section as part of a fairly consistent board agenda to conduct normal business decisions, board information updates, decisions, and adoption of resolutions.

As your board agenda is developed, your directors will rely on you to draft an agenda of what you consider to be relevant topics to review with your board. This draft should be reviewed and discussed with your lead independent director and board chair to ensure that the issues and concerns of the independent directors are addressed.

'Typical' Board Meeting Agenda Topics

There are several agenda topics that are relatively standard for any successful board meeting. These include a review of operational and financial performance, reviews of issues of importance to the board, committee reports, and resolutions. Additionally, I strongly recommend that two other topics be added to each board agenda: an executive session and an independent directors session. Good boards already have these topics on the agenda, but if your board doesn't, seriously consider adding them.

A successful board agenda might look like this:

I.   Executive Session
II.   Board Priority Topic
III.   Operational and Financial Performance Review
IV.   Updates on Relevant Issues Important to the Board
V.   Committee Reports
VI.   Resolutions
VII.   Independent Director Session

Let's look at each of these agenda items in more detail.

I. Executive Session

Setting the Stage

If you don't already do so, it's prudent to begin each of your board meetings with an executive session limited to directors and led by the CEO. Since you probably invite several members of your management team to be present during the discussion of other topics on the agenda, it may be difficult to discuss certain issues in front of them. Use the executive session as a platform to speak candidly, concisely, and privately to your directors about issues important to you. These may include personnel issues, specific comments you want to make about business performance, competitive activity, and any other issues that occupy significant amounts of your time and thought. This session permits you to disseminate important information to your board and frame issues that are important to you for their consideration. It provides your directors the opportunity to ask questions and provide ideas to help you work through these sometimes difficult issues.

Critical Success Factors

In my experience, there are several critical success factors to making this session effective. First, devote time before the meeting to thoughtfully craft the topics, discussion flow, and the information you will provide. Rambling monologues are a quick way to lose director interest and cause you to lose control of your agenda.

Your directors must learn to be patient, so that they listen, probe, and understand your comments. They need to pay close attention to you and listen carefully without passing immediate judgment or trying to solve your problems. Your directors need to use this time to understand your most important issues. They need to ask questions for clarification and understanding.

Finally, help them to understand what they are to do with this information. Are you providing it so that they have a better appreciation of presentations later in the meeting? Is it to provide additional perspective that your management team may be lacking? Is it to provide insight into an executive's performance that you might want the board to consider later in the meeting?

Benefits of a Good Executive Session

This part of the meeting can provide directors with excellent insight into your thought process, management, and communication styles. If you discuss a series of issues that are trivial or your discussion is unfocused, that tells them a lot about the way the company is being run. Conversely, if the issues are relevant, the communication succinct and comprehensive, they can gain an immediate sense that you have the company under tight control.

I have found that the executive session ranks among the most important parts of any board meeting. It requires a level of candor and trust from all board members that is a good indicator of the governance culture, overall governance process, and your relationship with the board. Sequentially successful executive sessions indicate a strong working relationship between you and the board. Poor executive sessions may be an indicator of deeper problems between you and the board or within the board.

When you seek feedback at the end of each board meeting, it's wise to always ask for specific feedback on the quality and value of the executive session.

II. Board Priority Topic

This agenda item permits an annual, in-depth rotating discussion of one of the four board priorities discussed in chapters 2-5. There are two effective ways to discuss these important subjects: The first is to devote a significant portion of the board agenda to one topic. This can easily be two to three hours for a good discussion. Another approach that has worked well is to use a board dinner the night before the board meeting to discuss the topic in detail. Overnight, allow the board members to reflect on what they heard. Then at the board meeting the next day, spend quality time reflecting on what was discussed and agreeing how to proceed.

Both approaches can be used effectively; which option to use is up to you and the board. Whatever path you chose, the information to review should be sent to the board well in advance of the meeting so the directors have a chance to thoroughly review and understand the information.

A prototype of an annual board calendar to discuss these rotating board priority topics might be something like this:

January:	Operating Plan Review
April:	Risk Management
July:	Strategy Review
October:	CEO Succession Planning and Management Development

III. Operational and Financial Performance Review

How Are We Doing?

One of the important topics discussed at every board meeting is the company's operational performance. Put simply, how are you doing versus your approved operating plan? A succinct quarterly review of the operating performance is an integral part of your responsibility to your board for several reasons.

First, your approved plan is a commitment by you and your management team to create value for your shareholders. From a governance standpoint, your board needs to assess whether value is being created as planned. If not, what are your remedial plans to create the expected value?

Second, the quarterly operating discussions provide a continuous flow of information on the state of the business, execution capability, competitive activity, pricing issues, and customer satisfaction. Your board cannot effectively fulfill its role without current information and understanding on important operational issues and performance.

Third, without current information, the directors cannot use their experience and expertise to help you and your management team. This is one of the board's primary responsibilities—to help and support their CEO.

Overall, the operating performance discussion is part review of performance, part education for the board, and part board support and coaching of you and your team. It's difficult to keep these separate and distinct, and sometimes one dominates. But a robust board discussion includes all three components.

Focusing the Discussion

Your fundamental challenge is to manage and lead this discussion so that it is as succinct and productive as possible. The starting point, as we discussed earlier is a thoughtful operating plan with clear measurable criteria and specific benchmarks that will be achieved each quarter. This seems logical, but failure to devote the time to discussing and agreeing upon these measurements upfront causes much wasted time later.

Measurable criteria used to assess performance include the obvious financial reports like the P&L, cash flow statement, and balance sheet. These are standard for all boards and all companies. The best way to manage these discussions is for you and your CFO to crystallize your operating review into a crisp thirty-minute presentation that covers the performance highlights. To keep performance in perspective, it's important that the board not only understand the performance of the past quarter but also year-to-date and estimates for the next quarter and the balance of the year.

Additionally, as discussed in chapter 2, if you and your board have agreed upon a series of key performance indicators, they will help keep this part of the agenda on track. Using a stoplight process, green is on or ahead of plan, yellow is a bit behind plan, and red is well off plan. Tracking the KPIs helps your directors to visually understand performance and focus the discussion on the most important indicators of performance.

Leverage and Develop Your Management Team

Any relevant discussion of your operating performance requires participation from key management executives in finance, sales, marketing, product development, and human resources. These leaders need to be available to answer questions and provide additional insight to the board. They also can receive direct feedback and suggestions from board members whose experience may prove valuable. When things are going well, some compliments from the board can be a very powerful motivator. When results are off plan, some pointed questions or comments from the board can provide a powerful incentive to improve performance.

The key to making these discussions as productive as possible is to focus the discussions on the most important issues and provide information to the board members well in advance of the meeting.

IV. Updates on Issues Important to the Board

At every board meeting, there are always issues important to your board. These are usually informational but can sometimes require a board decision. Topics might include things like a follow-up on a topic from a previous board meeting, preliminary thinking about a potential acquisition or divestiture, a legal proceeding, new technology development, and so forth. The selection criteria should be topics that the CEO thinks are important for the board to be aware of or important to good board governance.

There are no hard and fast rules for choosing these issues. Over time, you can develop an effective process for obtaining feedback from your board on important topics that will make the best use of their time. Your lead independent director and board chair are excellent resources to help you decide what to include and what topics can be handled by other means.

One effective way to use this portion of the agenda is to succinctly report progress back to your board on actions that were agreed to at previous meetings. Periodic updates on progress versus commitments provide an increased level of confidence and solidify your relationship with the board.

V. Committee Reports

At the full board meeting, each committee chair provides a summary of the discussions of their committee meeting and the important topics of which the full board needs to be aware and understand. Since each independent director serves on one or possibly two committees, some of the reports are redundant for them but are invaluable to those board members who are not on that committee. Effectively implemented, the committee reports make the best use of director time.

For your purposes, the committee reports are a summary of what you have already heard if you attended the individual meetings. More important, you get to hear the committee chairs articulate their comments and issues to the full board and see the reaction from other directors. Individual committee issues can easily frame follow-up discussions for future board or committee meetings.

VI. Resolutions

This section is usually perfunctory to provide legal documentation for board decisions. However, it's important that each resolution have the opportunity to be fully vetted and discussed before any vote. This means that you need to provide adequate background material, and sufficient time must be scheduled for ample discussion and deliberation. This reflects on the duty of care with which each director is charged.

Good CEOs ensure that their directors are well-versed on the background for the resolutions, and they devote the time to understanding and addressing any director concerns. It's sometimes valuable to speak with individual directors prior to board meetings to address their questions or concerns. Many times the routine appearance of approving some board resolutions is an indicator of the time you spent before the vote gaining consensus and agreement.

VII. Independent Director Session

Over the last several years, most boards have decided that to ensure independence and improved governance, they would have an independent directors' session at each board meeting. These sessions provide a valuable forum for your independent directors to speak candidly about any issues or concerns they have as the result of full-board or committee discussions. A lead director presides at these meetings and solicits issues and feedback from the independent directors. The lead director orchestrates follow-up discussion on important topics discussed during the formal board meeting.

These sessions are also beneficial in identifying issues that the board would like you to address at the next board meeting, issues that require further information, or issues requiring your immediate attention. During these sessions, the lead director also collects specific feedback on the board meeting, which will be shared with you.

It may appear to be counterintuitive, but I would encourage you to support and include adequate time for one of these sessions at the conclusion of each board meeting. Why would I suggest this since you're not there to defend yourself and provide your point of view?

My experience has shown that these independent director sessions can provide significant and valuable feedback to you if they are structured correctly. This benefit is derived from focusing the independent director discussions on a select group of questions posed by the lead independent director:

1. What feedback would you like to provide the CEO on the issues discussed at the board meeting?
2. Are there any other comments from directors on the key topic of board focus that was discussed?
3. Are there any concerns that you failed to express during the meeting or concerns that you don't believe that management heard or understood?
4. Are there any topics that should be included in the next board meeting?

This list is just a beginning, but these four questions can provide you with considerable insight and feedback that might be otherwise difficult to obtain. The lead director, if chosen properly, will have the skills to involve each independent director in the discussions and make sure that their input is obtained. Then he or she can provide that feedback to you after the meeting so that small issues or concerns don't fester and become big problems.

Demand Focus

Once the independent directors have agreed on the focus and priorities of the board and committees, they should share it with the full board and management so that there is total clarity and understanding. This clarity makes it easier for you to organize board agendas and provide the necessary information to meet board and individual director expectations. It also provides you and your team with a roadmap for planning to meet their needs. Finally, it keeps all board members focused on specific topics because they have confidence that other important issues will be addressed in due time.

Information Is Key

Effectiveness of a board begins with the quality and quantity of information the directors receive. It is vital that each board member have the information required to understand the company's business and issues. Where board decisions are required, it is critical that the issues be framed clearly, with relevant background information, options reviewed with pros and cons, and a management recommendation. Your board will look to you to provide a thoughtful recommendation based on facts rather than just delegate the problem or issue to the board for resolution.

Materials should be sent to the board five days in advance of committee and board meetings to allow for adequate time for review. It is difficult for the board to fulfill its responsibilities and be helpful to you unless there is adequate time to review materials before meetings. If one or two members are not well-versed in the information or have inadequate time to reflect on it, the quality of board discussions can be diminished, and the board will not function as effectively.

Make Your Team Accessible

An effective CEO and board relationship also requires open access of individual directors to management. There are two methods to achieve this valuable interaction. The first is to invite key management to regularly attend selected portions of your board meetings. The second is to encourage personal one-on-one contact between managers and individual board members.

At each board meeting, particularly during the operating performance review section of the agenda, your board will find it valuable to have the heads of sales, marketing, R&D, manufacturing, human resources, and finance present. These individuals are close to the day-to-day action and can provide additional insight into the business, competitive environment and financial performance. Discussions are greatly enhanced by these individuals' formal presentations on specific issues and their availability to answer questions. Your board will get to see them in action, presenting, and answering director questions. This provides the directors with additional perspective for succession planning discussions. Each of your executives will benefit from a better understanding of how the board functions, director issues, and overall board dynamics.

Board members have the right and fiduciary duty to talk to management to learn about your business and discuss issues of importance to the board. They also need to get to know your management team individually, so that they can have informed views when they discuss organization structure and succession planning issues. However, individual contact between your executives and directors should not be distracting to your management team or disruptive to your authority.

Normally, committee chairs and committee members have periodic contact with key members of management to fulfill their committee responsibilities.

For example, it would be expected that the audit committee chair and members would be in frequent contact with the CFO, and the directors of finance, internal audit, and tax to fulfill their committee responsibilities. On a higher level, there is great benefit for board members to periodically discuss broader issues with management team members. These can include strategic issues, competitive activity, and their personal development. To ensure that the proper protocol is in place, directors should advise your office of all personal contact or visits on these broader issues. You should assist in arranging the meetings. This will ensure that you are aware of any contact and that board members are not interfering in normal business activities.

Continuously Educate Your Board

To help you succeed as CEO, you must make sure that your directors are competent to fulfill their duties as a director. Hopefully, you have a diverse group of directors with the necessary skills and experience to help you with the business issues you face. As I discussed in chapter 8, if you're missing important skills or experiences on your board, work with your nominating and governance committee to fill these gaps.

For your current directors, continuously make sure that they understand the key operating issues, main sources of business risk, perceptions of stakeholders and investors, and the competitive environment in which you operate. The more knowledgeable they are, the better able they are to help you work on the important issues you face.

Make sure that your board understands your vision, priorities, and key areas of focus. Encourage face-to-face meetings with your executive team, site visits, and ongoing education for each director.

Summary

Today, more than ever, it is necessary for you to work with your board to achieve a collegial and comfortable working environment that accommodates robust and constructive discussion and debate. This begins with open communication and complete transparency. You must establish and maintain credibility. Your directors must believe in you and what you tell them.

The balance you must strike is between optimism and enthusiasm with openness and honesty. Create an atmosphere in which it is acceptable to bring problems to your board for discussion, and solicit their help if you don't have all the answers. Structure discussions so that everyone is heard. It is permissible to have divergent opinions, but consensus decisions can still be made swiftly.

Chapter Ten
Managing Potential Tensions

Evolving governance practices have the potential to periodically create tensions between CEOs and their boards. Even when a strong and positive relationship exists, tensions might develop. The intensity of these will ebb and flow over time depending on business results, market conditions, individual personalities, and the chemistry between the CEO and the board.

Understanding the background and reason for a specific tension does not diminish or eliminate it, but it only helps to explain it. Your job as CEO is to detect tensions early and manage them with your board so that ultimately they are reduced or eliminated.

I have categorized the tensions I have personally observed into eight categories. You may experience additional ones or you might not experience any or all of them. However, should you begin to experience one of these tensions, you'll be able to eliminate it through better understanding and using the lessons from others.

Tension #1: CEO Support Versus Critical Questioning

Boards usually try to be supportive of their CEO. A good board provides guidance and council on operational problems, strategy, and personnel issues. They provide access to business contacts and other areas of expertise that would be valuable to a CEO's success.

Today however, many CEOs are experiencing more probing questions at board meetings. Directors are questioning business performance, strategy, and the capabilities of the management team. Some CEOs fear voicing concern or dismay about these questions, but their body language at times conveys a feeling that they are no longer trusted or that the board is concerned with their performance. After particularly intense questioning, a CEO may even believe that the board has lost confidence in him or her.

More intense and focused questions from the board are a result of their need to better understand your business and competitive environments and assess performance. Directors need to ensure that they understand the relevant business issues, that alternatives have been thoughtfully considered, and that the decisions and strategies they have approved at past meetings are being implemented.

Don't assume that your board is out to get you. View your board's questions and probing from a positive perspective. They are not trying to find where you are failing or what you are doing wrong. In executing their fiduciary responsibility, they are trying to ensure that you and your team are doing everything possible to create value for your shareholders. They have insight and experience that can be very helpful to you and your management team.

Tension #2: High Level Operational Reviews Versus Micromanagement

Many board meetings now focus much more on critical measurements of a company's operational performance and how that performance affects business strategy. Boards are no longer content to just accept the high level results of quarterly performance but want to understand more about the drivers of current performance and the early indicators of future business performance. Increased time is being allocated at board meetings to discuss business strategy and how it is affected by short-term business results and competitive response.

I have seen CEOs interpret some of these detailed business oversight questions as micromanagement. In some cases, they were correct, and a director probed minutia that added little to the discussions. When this happens, a CEO tactfully needs to make his or her board aware that they are too far down into details. However, in some cases, detailed questions from directors are appropriate.

Remember that board members are not involved in the daily operations of your business and may not know what information is most relevant. Continual discussion with your board and agreement on what information should be provided and reviewed along with the KPIs discussed in chapter 2 can alleviate some of this tension and get everyone focused on the correct information and issues.

Tension #3: Short Term Focus Versus Long Term Strategy

Over the last several years, boards have increased their focus on monitoring the achievement of short-term quarterly commitments. Many CEOs want their boards to focus more on the long term. In reality, for CEOs and boards to be effective, there needs to be focus on both the short term and long term. Effective management of your board means that the CEO is achieving proper balance between the two.

Directors need to make sure that each quarterly commitment is achieved consistent with the approved annual operating plan and your long-term strategic plan. You and your board should view the short and long term not as mutually exclusive but as different points on the journey of continuous value creation for shareholders.

Tension #4: Compliance Oversight Versus Business Issues

An important duty of today's board is to ensure regulatory compliance. Many CEOs are concerned that board discussions are too focused on monitoring the mandated regulatory compliance to the detriment of important business issues. This compliance focus can be frustrating for a CEO. As part of its fiduciary responsibility, a board must be assured that your financial and operational processes are being adhered to and are well controlled.

The value of compliance is clear. There is no upside in a company's market capitalization for compliance to SOX or other financial reporting requirements. However, if there are material SOX compliance weaknesses, a failure to file financial reports on time, or worse, a restatement of financials, market capitalization can easily decrease by 20 percent or more.

You and your board would not be performing your duties if there were not a continuous focus on both regulatory compliance and business issues. As CEO, you need to work with your board to make sure that discussions of regulatory compliance are balanced with substantive business issue discussions.

Tension #5: Plan Review Versus Plan Development

Finding the right balance between plan review and plan development has been an area of increased tension on many boards. In the past, your board may have just quickly reviewed the annual operating plan and the long-term strategy. Now, some CEO's are claiming that their boards want to play a much more active role as these plans are developed. Indeed, this may be the case on boards that are tending to micromanage the CEO.

As CEO, your job is to manage the discussions, so that directors have the proper information to discuss your plans and provide suggestions for improvement. As you manage the planning process, you need to make sure that your board understands the market and competitive business background, key assumptions, financial plan, and proposed investments. If managed correctly, board questions should not be perceived as developing the plan but rather as a part of a process to help you develop the best possible plan. A strong CEO and board relationship uses all the resources and experience necessary to develop the best possible operating and strategic plans to create value for stockholders.

Tension #6: Leadership Development and Succession Planning

CEO succession planning and leadership development are important roles for both you and the board. The annual board review of these plans should include fact-based discussions about each of the individuals involved, including their strengths, weaknesses, and potential to assume additional responsibility.

You work with these individuals daily and see everything while your board only sees them quarterly. The board relies heavily on your assessment and proposal for your succession. However, over time each board member will form independent views on the performance, potential, leadership skills, and capability to assume additional responsibility of each member of your management team.

Do not perceive board member opinions that differ from your assessment as a negative. Instead, think of any differences as an added set of observations and data points that can help you develop and lead your team more effectively. When CEO succession occurs, the board has the final decision rights, but it needs your input and recommendation. If the process works effectively, there should be no surprises when the board makes these important succession decisions.

Tension #7: Risk Management

The discussion of risk management at the board level is continually evolving. However, it has the potential to breed tension between CEOs and their boards. In regulatory filings like the 10-K and 10-Qs, you and your management team have identified multiple areas of business risk that could affect the performance of your business. Originally, these were identified to meet regulatory disclosure requirements. However, over the past couple of years, these risks have been continually refined to reflect the true risks that are relevant to your business.

Increased tension arises when the board begins to question how you are addressing these risks. You may conclude that the board is micromanaging your business or trying to protect themselves from any potential legal liability that might exist. However, I suggest that you think about risk management oversight in a much different way.

If the risks are sufficiently serious that a potential investor should be aware of them, why shouldn't they be a board issue? As investors look for improved governance and oversight, why shouldn't the board be held accountable for an acceptable level of operational, strategic and reputational risk oversight? Why shouldn't your board, as representatives of the investors, have the right to probe each risk and satisfy themselves that you and your management team are doing everything prudent to understand and mitigate these risks? Is this really micromanagement or prudent board governance?

Tension #8: CEO-Board Collegiality Versus Independence

In the new governance environment, there is a fine line that needs to be drawn in your relationship with the board. Interactions and meetings need to be collaborative and collegial for maximum effectiveness. At the same time, all interactions need to maintain a level of independence to achieve good governance. The difficult question is where you and the board draw this line.

If you're too collegial, you can easily fall into the same trap as the CEO and board relationships before the recent spate of corporate scandals. No one asks the difficult and provocative questions. Worse, no one asks follow-up questions to bore down into the details. Conversely, if your board too independent, it might achieve good governance but at the expense of a poor relationship with you and your team. Every interaction then has the potential to become confrontational. Communications can suffer and information flow to the board may be constrained. Bad business decisions will result.

You need to work with your board to find the proper balance. How can board interactions be collegial but still accommodate difficult questions and disagreements? One of the true hallmarks of a successful relationship between a CEO and his or her board is how disagreements are discussed and decisions made when there are dissenting opinions.

Summary

When one examines all the tensions, it's easy to see how any one of these potential tension areas can strain the relationship between you and the board or with individual directors. In combination, unresolved tensions can easily create a seriously strained working relationship. In reality, you and your board face the challenge to jointly find the right balance for each of these tensions. A tension not managed properly can rapidly become counterproductive to effective leadership and good corporate governance. As CEO, it is critical to take an active role in managing discussions on these tensions as they develop and to find a mutually agreeable solution to effectively manage the tension.

PART THREE:

IMPROVING YOUR BOARD RELATIONSHIP

Chapter Eleven
Building on Your Success

Continuous monitoring of how well you're relating to your board is critical to your success as CEO. Assuming you have agreed with the board on priorities and how they will evaluate your performance, continual feedback is mandatory.

The All-Important Feedback Loop

This feedback can come from several sources. Formal feedback from your lead director after an independent directors' session provides immediate information on how you're doing. Conversations with individual directors can occur at any time between board meetings. As you talk to individual directors on specific business issues, take the opportunity to weave feedback opportunities into your discussion. An annual formal appraisal process, supplemented with semiannual or quarterly feedback, provides specific fact-based responses on agreed objectives and performance standards. Finally, based on your own observations, you can perform a self-assessment using some or all of the questions posed in the appendix.

Regardless of the final process you use, each of these feedback vehicles is useful. When used together, they become a powerful tool to monitor your performance and board relationship.

Establish the Right Environment

From the beginning, clearly establish your desire for honest feedback so you can do your job better. Through your actions and comments, demonstrate you want and value board feedback. Listen carefully to what your directors are telling you without becoming defensive. If your directors see you establishing a culture of continual learning and acting on their feedback to improve, they will become even more supportive of your efforts.

Board Issues and Director Concerns

It is important that you listen carefully to director concerns and issues. Understand what they are telling you. If you agree with them, act on their recommendations. If you disagree, take the time to explain your position and try to reach agreement with them. It is dangerous to ignore their concerns. This can easily lead to an impasse, and, eventually, the board will probably win the disagreement.

It is difficult to work successfully with your board if there are major areas of unresolved disagreement. These issues can slowly fester and eventually can create an irreparable rift between you and the board.

You can continually do a quick check of director sentiment in your normal director interactions by using the following three questions.

- Am I focused on the right areas?
- What issues do you see arising in the next twelve months that I should be looking at?
- Are there any important issues where the board and I are not in alignment?

Feedback on Your Performance

Each year, it is important that the board, with input from each director, evaluate your performance. Agreement on the criteria and process the board will use to assess your performance is one of the most important topics on which to agree with the board. It is your right to know the board's expectations and how they will measure your performance.

Fundamentally, you should be able to answer the following question clearly and concisely: How will the board evaluate my performance, communications, and leadership style?

There should be a clear process to assess your performance against a defined set of financial and nonfinancial criteria. These measurements will be both quantitative and qualitative. You should be prepared to provide your own self-assessment and review it with those directors charged with discussing and assessing your performance.

Using Your Chairman and Lead Director

A nonexecutive chair or lead director can play an important role in providing feedback and also enhancing and facilitating communications between you and your board. It is critical that you and your lead director develop a close working relationship. Discuss your individual roles and how you can most effectively work together. As a starting point, reflect on the particular issues facing your company and how you can both effectively work on these issues.

A lead director must have the respect and trust of the other independent directors and the CEO to work effectively. Often, communication between a board member or between the board and the CEO may become strained. The board members and the CEO must feel that the lead director will be able to help resolve outstanding issues while maintaining trust and integrity at all times.

The lead director must also exhibit other requisite skills such as the ability to efficiently run meetings. He or she must listen well to all viewpoints, draw out opinions from each director, and synthesize positive and negative feedback into actionable items. The lead director must not be afraid to challenge you as CEO and have respectful but direct conversations with you if you and the board differ on important issues.

Since time at board meetings is limited, productive use of the board's time is critical for success. The lead director can play an important role in helping to structure agendas and suggest relevant board materials to ensure constructive discussions of important issues. This usually requires a substantial amount of work before board meetings and a close working relationship with you.

As discussed earlier, time should be allotted at the conclusion of each board meeting for a discussion between independent directors without the CEO present. These independent director discussions tend to be a bit more open and candid than board meetings and frequently elicit comments from all directors, even those who say little during formal board meetings. They also provide directors with the opportunity to digest what they have heard during the board meeting and collect their thoughts on the feedback they want to provide to you.

For an effective CEO and board relationship, it's important that a mechanism be developed to provide feedback to you as soon after the board meeting as practical. This feedback process should be clear and consistent, either through the lead director, nonexecutive chair, or a senior board member. You must be confident that the person providing the feedback is truly representing the board and not focused on personal agendas.

Use this person as a valuable resource to help you understand individual board members and build better relationships with the board and with each director. You can also use your lead director to communicate any sensitive issues to the independent directors. For example, if you think that the board is interfering too much in strategy development, use your lead director to work through that issue for you.

Build on Your Success

As you acquire feedback on what is going right and what areas can be improved, you'll likely need some course corrections in your plan and behavior. There is not one formula for success that fits all CEO and board relationships. The best CEOs I have seen continually build on their successes and work on continuous improvement of their board relationship.

The feedback you receive should be mostly positive with some areas for improvement. Use the positive feedback as a springboard to improve. This will demonstrate to the board your commitment to self-improvement and also how you value the feedback they provide.

Change Will Be Continual

One of the most interesting observations I have made over the years is the continual change in CEO and board relationships. In hindsight, the changes were absolutely predictable. However, I had to experience them firsthand to understand their importance and the need for a CEO to continually implement many of the concepts in this book.

Changes in your relationship with the board will be driven by many external and internal factors. These factors operate independently but sometimes simultaneously to create a fluid and dynamic situation.

Let's take a look at some of the factors causing the change.

1. Corporate governance standards are in a constant state of change because of legal and regulatory mandates combined with implementing the best practices of board governance.
2. Board membership will most likely change during your tenure as CEO. Each new director has the potential to significantly alter board dynamics. He or she brings new expertise, perhaps a different perspective, and most likely a different director style.
3. Many boards rotate committee assignments. As directors serve on different committees, their issues, perspectives, and experience will affect committee dynamics and ultimately board dynamics.
4. You are changing! Each day, you are growing and developing your skills as a CEO. You are also continually applying your knowledge to interact differently with the board.

Each of these factors can be positive and provide new opportunities for improving your relationship with the board. However, you cannot afford to become complacent because change can negatively affect the relationship if you don't anticipate it and act promptly.

Ensuring You Have the Right Directors

Have the courage to recruit directors who will challenge you and help you grow and succeed. A fundamental principle of successful leadership is being surrounded with the right people. The same goes for directors.

Seek diversity in the areas of competence, complimentary skills, experience, style, and thought process. Diversity leads to richer board discussions and better counsel for you. Good directors are results oriented, strategic, collaborative, and independent.

You're Running a Marathon

One way to view building a successful relationship with your board is to compare it to running a marathon. You have trained well and have learned the requisite skills. Both you and the directors have started at the same place at the same time, but over time, you are at different points on the marathon course. Some of your directors, based on experience on other boards, may already have completed the first marathon and are now running a second one.

Do not minimize the need to continuously work on building positive relationships with the board. Implementing the fundamental concepts outlined in this book is vital to your success as a CEO.

Summary

A wise CEO takes the lead in developing and managing a strong board relationship. Devote quality time to understanding your board. Continually communicate with them individually and as a full board. They are there to help you. They aren't your enemy or a necessary evil. The time you invest communicating with them and listening to their questions and concerns facilitates a positive and productive working relationship.

Take time periodically to think about the major issues you are facing, and make sure you have the proper skills and experience on the board to help you. Your input to the nominating and governance committee is critical to maintaining the correct skill set on the board, particularly as your business changes.

Should tension develop between you and the board or individual board members, address it immediately. It's always best to tackle a tension earlier rather than to let it fester and become a major issue.

Realize that you and the directors are on a long journey with no clear road-map for continuing governance success. Each of you may be at different places on the journey because of your varied experiences. Take the time to continually discuss oversight and governance issues with them. Always make sure that you understand their expectations and be sure to clearly voice any issues or concerns with them.

Use your lead director or nonexecutive chairman as a facilitator and valuable asset to interface with the board. Use this position to frame issues; prioritize; obtain feedback; and provide counsel. The lead director is also an excellent channel for communicating difficult messages from you to the board or individual members.

Finally, your directors are busy and are not spending the same amount of time that you do on your business. Don't assume they are totally versed in all your business issues, performance, and all the market dynamics that affect your strategy. Continually communicate and confirm their level of understanding.

Being an effective and successful CEO requires hard work and building strong relationships with many constituencies. In the midst of all the conflicting demands placed on you, don't forget to invest time on managing your board.

Finally, use the questions in the appendix for personal reflection, to help organize your thoughts and to develop effective strategies.

Appendix A

Questions for Personal Reflection
Key Areas of Board Focus

The following questions are useful for reflecting about your current board relationship. The questions can be used in multiple ways. You can use them in a particular subject area to periodically reflect and thoughtfully evaluate your performance. Should there be a particular problem or tension you're trying to personally resolve with the board, use the questions that relate to that issue as the basis for self-reflection and action planning.

Annual Operating Plan

Have my board and I agreed on the measurements and key performance indicators that we will use to monitor business performance at each board meeting?

Do I focus board reviews of operating performance on these measurements to help focus discussions on the most relevant operating issues?

How does the board feel about my annual operating plan in terms of aggressiveness, resourcing, and probability of success?

Have the board and I agreed that we have the necessary resources to achieve our goals?

How does the board feel about the operational and financial controls I have in place?

Business Strategy

Does my board understand our market, our competitive position, and the strategies I have to increase shareholder value?

Have the board and I agreed on the strategies and investments that will create long-term value for our shareholders?

Do I provide periodic strategy updates as market conditions change?

Succession Planning

Am I spending an appropriate amount of time with the board on succession planning for my position and succession for key members of my management team?

How well do the directors know my potential successors?

Have the board and I agreed that I have the right organization structure in place?

How does my board view the performance and potential of each member of my senior management team?

Risk Management

How well does my board understand and agree on the key risks facing my business?

How well does my board understand how I am managing these risks?

Have I consistently sought board input to strengthen my risk management plans?

If there have been significant changes in the risk profile of my business, have I informed the board in a timely manner?

Board Composition and Dynamics

Do my directors, in aggregate, possess the right mix of skills and business experience to help me address the current issues facing the company?

As I look to the issues I will be working on in the next few years, are there any critical skills and experience that my directors lack?

Is my relationship and interaction with my directors conducive to open communication and meaningful participation in board discussions?

How do I routinely provide feedback to my board on their performance?

Appendix B

Questions for Personal Reflection
Five Fundamental Principles

The introduction to this book describes **Five Fundamental Principles** derived from observing how effective CEOs manage their boards as well as lessons from those who have made rookie mistakes.

1. Understand your board's focus and expectations.
2. Provide timely, accurate, and relevant information to your directors.
3. Establish effective two-way communication with your board and individual directors.
4. Develop a robust, continual personal assessment and feedback process.
5. Use continual change as an opportunity to enhance your board relationship.

These principles, when implemented successfully, will help you create a strong and effective governance process and make for a positive and powerful relationship between you and your board.

Use the following questions to help you reflect on the current status of your board knowledge and relationship. For any areas that can be improved, use the ideas in this book to develop clear and concise personal action plans.

1. Understand your board's focus and expectations

Chapters 1 through 8 described the focus, governance implications, expectations, and importance of the entire board, as well as each committee. List your understanding of the priorities for your board and for each of the board committees.

Has my board and each of our committees clearly defined their priorities and focus for the current year?

How well do I understand board focus and priorities?

How well do I understand the function, focus, and expectations of each of the board's committees?

How well do I understand the board's (full board and its committees) governance processes?

Have the board and I agreed upon the process to discuss one of the key areas of board focus (chapters 2-5) each time we meet?

How will I periodically verify this information and ensure that my understanding is always current?

2. Provide timely, accurate, and relevant information to your directors

The information and resources available to your board are critical to effective governance as well as providing the most help to make you successful.

Have I confirmed with my directors that the information they are receiving is sufficient for them to fulfill their fiduciary responsibilities and help me with my business issues?

Am I providing relevant information to my board in the right format and with sufficient time for thoughtful review?

Does each director understand the key operating issues of my business?

Does each director understand the main sources of risk to my company?

Do I provide my board with independent analytical reports and sources of information to help them better understand my business and competitive issues?

Do I provide my board access to my management team, so they can better understand key issues and get to know these leaders better?

3. Establish effective two-way communication with your board and individual directors.

The chemistry and interaction between you and the board needs to be open, honest, and candid. How will I ensure that my interactions with the board and individual directors are conducive to meaningful participation and open two-way dialogue?

Are my agendas for each board and committee meeting planned properly to effectively and efficiently meet director priorities?

Are discussions with my board open and candid?

How well am I using my time during the executive session?

Do board discussions provide the proper level of director interaction with members of my management team?

Do board discussions strike the proper balance of short-term operating performance balanced properly with broader strategic issues?

What tensions am I currently experiencing with the board? How am I addressing these tensions?

How can I improve the frequency of communication and ongoing dialogue with my board and individual directors?

Do the directors believe there is sufficient level of contact between themselves and senior members of my leadership team?

4. Develop a robust, continual personal assessment and feedback process

Knowing how the board views your performance, their level of satisfaction with the information they receive, and the quality of their interaction with you are all vital to a successful long-term relationship. What processes and techniques will you use to get timely and actionable feedback from your board?

Do I receive quality feedback from my board after each board meeting and independent directors' session?

Are there consistent issues in this feedback that indicate an opportunity for improvement?

Have my board and I agreed upon a clear set of measurement criteria to evaluate my performance?

Overall, how well (quality, quantity, and timeliness) do I get feedback from the board on my performance?

5. Use continual change as an opportunity to enhance your board relationship

The only thing that is certain is change. How will you stay abreast of new governance issues, changing expectations, and evolving interpersonal dynamics so you are responsive to the needs of your board?

How do I track and assess the impact of any changes that are occurring in board interactions?

What changes have I observed in my interactions with the board in the last six months, and how have I responded?

Have there been any changes in focus or new issues with which my board and committees are dealing?

Acknowledgements

All books have shortcomings and in this time of rapidly evolving corporate governance, I'll take full responsibility for any in this book. The lessons in this book have been distilled from observing and working with a number of outstanding corporate executives and board directors. I'd like to acknowledge just a few of them.

I would like to thank George Conrades, Executive Chairman of Akamai Technologies for his encouragement to write this book, his thoughtful comments on early drafts and initially suggesting in 2003 that I be a lead director of his company. He is a visionary leader and a great personal mentor who has helped me to become a better director during my association with him.

Three individuals took time from their very busy schedules to review drafts of this book and provide insightful comments and suggestions. Geoffrey Moore, a noted author and business strategist, provided valuable support and counsel in reviewing and structuring the content of this book. Fred Salerno has been a role model director always freely sharing his insights and experience as a director on many diverse boards. Mike Duffy, CEO of OpenPages provided insight and critical review that helped to improve the clarity of lessons and practical plans proposed in this book.

Earlier in my career, I had the honor of working with two outstanding directors on the Eastman Kodak board. John Phelan, Retired Chairman

& CEO of the New York Stock Exchange was a prototypical lead director well before the concept was ever formally discussed in governance circles. On the same board, Paul O'Neill, retired Chairman & CEO of Alcoa, asked the most penetrating and insightful questions that I have ever witnessed on a corporate board. Both men, through their example, questions and mentoring helped me develop skills and experiences that have stood the test of time.

I have learned from each of the executives and directors I have ever been associated with. Thank you all. Some, by their example have provided valuable insights into establishing a very successful relationship between the CEO and board. Others have not been so successful. Both groups have provided the learnings and insights I have tried to share with you in this book.

Finally, I would like to thank my wife Patrice who has had the patience and tenacity to raise our six sons while I spent a large part of my time pursuing my passion for business leadership and continuously learning.

September 2009

Author Biography

Martin M. Coyne II is a professional board director and senior advisor to CEOs, boards of directors, and investors, and the author of many articles on board governance issues, improving the effectiveness of CEOs, and board/CEO relationships. A director of Akamai Technologies since November 2001, he was named Lead Director in May 2003. He also serves on the boards of OpenPages and Avecia Group Plc. Prior to his retirement, the author was Executive Vice President of Eastman Kodak, as well as Chairman of the Board of Welch Allyn, and board member of Advanced Medical Technology Association (AdvaMed), where he also served on the Executive and International committees. He earned his B.S. from Fordham University, his MBA from Fairleigh Dickinson University, and attended the Advanced Management Program at the Wharton School of Business.